Thrive

Also by Dan Buettner

The Blue Zones: Lessons for Living Longer
From the People Who've Lived the Longest

Thrive

Finding Happiness
the Blue Zones Way

Dan Buettner

NATIONAL GEOGRAPHIC

WASHINGTON, D.C.

Published by the National Geographic Society

ISBN: 978-1-4262-0818-8
First paperback printing 2011
ISBN: 978-1-4262-0515-6 (hardcover)

The National Geographic Society is one of the world's largest nonprofit scientific and educational organizations. Founded in 1888 to "increase and diffuse geographic knowledge," the Society's mission is to inspire people to care about the planet. It reaches more than 400 million people worldwide each month through its official journal, *National Geographic,* and other magazines; National Geographic Channel; television documentaries; music; radio; films; books; DVDs; maps; exhibitions; live events; school publishing programs; interactive media; and merchandise. National Geographic has funded more than 9,600 scientific research, conservation and exploration projects and supports an education program promoting geographic literacy. For more information, visit www.nationalgeographic.com.

For more information, please call 1-800-NGS LINE (647-5463) or write to the following address:

National Geographic Society
1145 17th Street N.W.
Washington, DC 20036-4688 U.S.A.

www.nationalgeographic.com

For information about special discounts for bulk purchases, please contact National Geographic Books Special Sales: ngspecsales@ngs.org.

For rights or permissions inquiries, please contact National Geographic Books Subsidiary Rights: ngbookrights@ngs.org

Cover Design: Melissa Farris
Interior Design: Cameron Zotter and Lindsey Smith

Printed in U.S.A.

11/QGF/1

To Spanky, Irene, and Rafa,
who, despite research that might suggest otherwise,
are a father's greatest source of happiness.

Contents

PREFACE   IX
Searching for Happiness

CHAPTER ONE   1
The Truth About Happiness

CHAPTER TWO   23
Denmark
The World's Happiness All-Stars

CHAPTER THREE   73
Singapore
Can You Manufacture a Happy Nation?

CHAPTER FOUR   127
Mexico
The Secret Sauce of Happiness

CHAPTER FIVE   173
San Luis Obispo
A Real American Dream

CHAPTER SIX   205
Lessons in Thriving

AFTERWORD   247

READING GROUP GUIDE   261

ACKNOWLEDGMENTS   271

BIBLIOGRAPHY   275

INDEX   277

Even after she turned 100, Francesca Castillo, called Panchita by her friends, kept cutting her own wood at her home on the Nicoya Peninsula in Costa Rica, reflecting a positive energy and happy outlook. PHOTO BY GIANLUCA COLLA

Searching for Happiness

It's ten o'clock on a Sunday morning in Hojancha, a small town in rural Costa Rica, and I'm on a mission. A few years ago, I met a woman here, the daughter of a Cuban revolutionary, who raised four children by herself on the edge of the jungle. Her name was Panchita, and when I first got to know her she had just celebrated her 99th birthday. Wearing a colorful dress, carnival beads, and hooped earrings, she would sit on a wooden plank on the patio of her tin-roofed house, dangle her legs above the dirt floor, and tell stories with friends and relatives who came to visit. She punctuated her conversations with a gentle touch and, depending on the topic, a sympathetic sigh or a whooping laugh. At sunset, once her guests had departed, she would make herself a simple meal of beans and handmade tortillas, say her prayers, and go to bed.

Recently I heard that Panchita had a medical setback and moved out of her farmhouse into a one-room shack behind her son's place. I'm on my way to see her now.

A modest community of cinder-block houses, shops, and stables, Hojancha is populated mainly by farmers and *sabaneros,* the leathery-tough cowboys of Central America. Set apart from the rest of Costa Rica on the Nicoya Peninsula, people here have been left to themselves to follow the rhythms of their Mesoamerican ancestors. Something about their lifestyle—perhaps the lime-soaked corn tortillas called *nixtamale,* the wildly exotic fruits they grow in their gardens, the off-the-charts levels of calcium and magnesium in their tap water, their ability to shed stress with laughter and conversation, or even their penchant for extramarital sex—has given people in this region the extraordinary gift of long life. In fact, the Nicoya Peninsula represents one of the most impressive pockets of longevity in the entire Western Hemisphere—a Blue Zone, as I've come to call such places. For the past eight years I've been studying the world's longevity Blue Zones. I've met more than 250 centenarians on five continents, some of whom still work as lawyers, stand on their heads, climb trees, or compete in karate matches.

Yet few have charmed me like Panchita.

When I arrive at her shack on this Sunday morning, the place is packed. A priest has come to say Catholic Mass, and others have stopped by to socialize, including middle-aged women from town, an 80-year-old cowboy, and a boy who used to corral Panchita's chickens for her when she lived alone. Sitting upright on her bed, she looks up at me through milky-rimmed pupils and, in a flash of recognition, yelps, *"¡Hola, Papi!"* She wraps me in a bony embrace and holds on. As I hug her back, feeling her warm, birdlike body, I realize that when this body was born, Mark Twain was still writing fiction, and construction had not yet begun on the *Titanic*. Positively beaming, she pulls me down next to her. "See, God has blessed me!" she brags to her guests. "El Gringo has come to visit me." And I'm thinking: Here's a 103-year-old woman who has no money and no real possessions, is living in a borrowed house, is half paralyzed and mostly blind, and she feels blessed that I've shown up? How is that possible?

LEARNING FROM THE EXPERTS

It's an eye-opening experience. During my years of studying longevity, I've visited Blue Zones in Sardinia; Okinawa; Loma Linda, California; the Greek island of Ikaría; and the Nicoya Peninsula—all places where people tend to suffer lower rates of heart disease and cancer than the rest of us and live up to a decade longer. Now I'm wondering if there might also be pockets of people like Panchita who hold the secrets to a *happier* life. Are there places around the globe that nurture happiness in the same way that the Blue Zones nurture longevity? If there are, what can we learn from these places to increase our own happiness in the same way that we've learned lessons about long life from the world's centenarians?

As I began to pursue this idea, I quickly discovered that an explosion of research in happiness studies has taken place during the past few decades. Social scientists, for example, have gathered a critical mass of data from thousands of worldwide surveys that not only pinpoint which nations experience the highest level of happiness and life satisfaction, but also begin to explain why—and some of the reasons aren't what you'd expect. In places where women have achieved gender equality, for instance, men tend to be happier than women. And in places where women are still not treated equally, women are often happier than men. Other studies have shown that, despite the popular belief that nobody wants to get older, most people actually get happier after a certain age. Clearly, the truth about happiness holds many surprises.

In fact, the deeper I dig into the research, the more apparent it becomes that happiness is a more complicated concept than longevity. Determining whether a person is 99 or 100 years old is a fairly straightforward task. But how do you measure how happy someone is? And what do we mean by happiness? Isn't happiness different for every person? How likely is it that even the world's top experts can come up with a neat prescription to help others become happier?

In the face of such challenges, it might be easy to dismiss happiness as a notion that's too elusive to pin down. But having seen with my own eyes how Panchita and others like her have metabolized a lifetime of hardship into their own brand of joy, I'm more convinced than ever that the true sources of happiness can't be revealed by scientific studies alone. We also need to consider the experiences of the happiness experts themselves—people who put theory into practice every day in pockets of well-being around the world.

THE WORLD'S HAPPIEST PLACES

In the pages that follow we'll visit four of the places identified by researchers as world leaders in happiness. The first is Denmark's Jutland Peninsula, where we'll meet some of the world's happiness all-stars. Next we'll go to the island nation of Singapore, whose citizens rank highest in Asia for happiness, despite living under the heavy hand of an authoritarian government. After that, we'll visit the Mexican state of Nuevo León, where people report being significantly happier than their much richer neighbors to the north. And finally we'll take a short trip to the town of San Luis Obispo in California to see how an American community has cooked up its own recipe for satisfaction in life.

As we explore each pocket where people are thriving in different ways, we'll see how culture, geography, and government policies combine to stack the deck in favor of happiness. Which types of governments yield the greatest happiness dividends for citizens? Which cultural values foster the greatest degree of life satisfaction? What role does religion play? How about money? What's the optimal mix of communal tradition and individual choice? What can the world's happiest peoples tell us about what makes a difference in their lives?

To find out, we'll start by plumbing the most comprehensive scientific databases—tens of millions of data points collected over the past 70 years and representing 95 percent of the world's population—to identify which beliefs, traditions, habits, and physical environments correlate most closely to happiness. In other words, which factors accompany happiness? Then we'll sit down with social scientists, economists, writers, demographers, physiologists, anthropologists, politicians, and even comedians to piece together the unique happiness formulas in each location. We'll get to know a real estate tycoon, a homemaker, a lawyer, a teacher, a prime minister, a businesswoman, a winemaker, a faith healer, a talk-show host, and a garbage man. All have stories that contribute to the bigger picture of happiness in their regions. Finally, informed by the latest scientific research, we'll distill the common denominators of satisfaction from each place to show you how to set up your own life to maximize happiness.

When I first set out to learn the secrets of long life, I discovered that the best way to do that was to identify the places where people lived the longest and then to study those places methodically, while making a special effort to absorb the wisdom of individuals who had lived long lives. I think the story of happiness is much the same. The best way to understand happiness is to focus on the remarkable people who rank themselves as very happy (at least an 8 on a scale of 10) and who also believe that they will be happier in the next five years—an optimistic condition that researchers describe as *thriving*.

As we'll see, the secret to achieving happiness in your own life lies in making subtle changes in your surroundings to create gentle but ever present nudges. This book will show you how. Think of it as a manual on how to set up your life so you can *thrive* in the same way that Panchita has—without really trying.

CHAPTER ONE

The Truth
About Happiness

What makes people happy? For many it's belonging to a club or social group, as 90 percent of Danes do. Rasmus Bjerner trains his champion rabbit outside Århus, Denmark, to compete at his local Rabbit Jumping Association. PHOTO BY DAVID McLAIN/AURORA

The Truth
About Happiness

Before we dig deeper into the nature of happiness, I'd like you to take a short quiz. I'm going to introduce you to three people I met during my travels, and I want you to tell me which one you think is happiest.

The first is Jan Hammer, a 42-year-old father of three girls who lives in Århus, the second largest city in Denmark. Each morning at three o'clock, his alarm clock rings, and he rolls out of the warm bed he shares with his wife of 15 years. He eats two fried eggs and toast, washes it down with a mug of coffee, and slips into a blaze orange jumpsuit. By four o'clock he's at the wheel of a high-tech garbage truck and is staring at a NASA-like dashboard with flashing buttons and multiple-view video screens. At each of 59 stops he jumps out of the cab and, with marmot-like zeal, trots from Dumpster to Dumpster and heaves fresh refuse into the hopper with the help of a hydraulic lift. "I don't even smell it anymore," he huffs, sweat seeping through his jumpsuit.

The second person is Norridah Yusoh, a 43-year-old housewife who lives with her husband and three school-age children in an apartment in Singapore. Each morning she dutifully puts on a head scarf, covering her hair as her religion requires; makes her children breakfast; prepares lunch for her husband, an accountant; and sends her family off for the day. After they're gone, she does household chores and, at midday, she might walk to a nearby food market, to buy food from various vendors and stop to chat along the way. Some nights after dinner, she goes to the local McDonald's, where she socializes with other Muslim mothers as her children nibble french fries and do homework. Then, each night before bed, as tradition dictates, she kisses her husband's hand to show respect.

The third person is Manuel Uribe, a 45-year-old Mexican man who lives in a working-class neighborhood of Monterrey. Manuel has a knack for trading, a soothing facility for conversation, and a sincere compassion. He's also a big man. In fact, a combination of bad genes and a taste for junk food has ballooned his weight to the point where he's confined to a bed in the living room of his mother's house. This doesn't impede visitors. On any given day, his room is abuzz with people seeking to cut a deal, to get advice, or just to experience a dollop of Manuel's charm. At noon, Manuel's mother brings out his lunch—a lean filet of meat and a generous helping of steamed broccoli. "It's from the Zone Diet," he says. "I've lost 200 pounds in the last year." Just then the door opens. Claudia Solis, a 30-something secretary, walks in on high heels. She puts a knee on the bed, cranes her lovely neck, and plants a pink-frosted kiss on Manuel's lips.

So what's the answer to the quiz? Which of these three people is the happiest? You've probably already guessed the answer: *All three of them are happy*—so happy, in fact, that, according to the latest research, they are almost certainly three of the happiest people in three of the happiest places on the planet.

How can that be?

Let's go back to the garbageman. I met Jan at six o'clock on a gray morning in the alley behind my hotel in Århus. He was emptying Dumpsters into his behemoth garbage truck. He greeted me heartily, and I could instantly tell that he was a nice guy. Pulling off a dirty cotton glove, he offered me his plump hand, which emitted the sweet-sour smell of his profession.

Later, seated in his cab, Jan punched the accelerator, and we sped through the misty Danish dawn. "You can't find a better job than delivering garbage," he whispered conspiratorially. "I work only 21 hours a week and make $80,000 a year. I drive a Mercedes and take my family to Greece each year." I looked over at him. He was wearing red square-rimmed glasses, Nike running shoes, and a bracelet that read "World's Most Beautiful Garbage Man." By eight o'clock he'd be done with his route and back at the garbage truck depot, he said. After a shower, he'd hit the gym and spa provided by his workers' union. Some days, he might go to a second job where he worked as a freelance bricklayer. There he would make another $60,000 a year.

More important than the money, though, was the satisfaction he felt with his life. "I'm like the yolk of the egg!" he said, using a Danish expression for "fat and happy." In his community, there was no stigma attached to the "garbage delivery" business. On weekends, he'd socialize with the dentists and lawyers who lived on his block. Home by three o'clock every afternoon, he had time to help his three daughters with their homework. Three nights a week he'd go to a local gym, where he'd put on shorts, sneakers, a red sports shirt, and a whistle to coach his daughters' indoor soccer team. His life was rewarding and full.

As for Norridah, listen to what she said when I asked her to rate her happiness on a scale of 1 to 10: "I'm a 9.5! I have a lot of friends from a wide variety of backgrounds." This was important for her, living in Singapore, because the government there strongly encourages harmony among the nation's three major ethnic groups: Chinese, Indians, and Malays such as Norridah. "Ever since my school days, I've mixed with Chinese and Indians and learned how to make friends with all of them," she said. "Maybe I talk most with my Malay friends on the phone, but when I go out—which I do every day—I meet my Indian friends at the market or play cards with Chinese friends. My children are the same way. They don't see color or race, they see people."

"How about your *tudong*?" I asked, using the Malay word for a head scarf. "You live in this modern city, your husband is an accountant, your kids listen to iPods. Your scarf seems so traditional. Do you feel you're free to take if off and show your hair, if you want?"

"That is my own choice," she said, gently passing her hand over the scarf. "It's part of our religion, and it is the way of our leaders. I choose to wear it. My daughter's generation might have different ideas. But it makes me comfortable, so I wear it."

"And how about this custom of kissing your husband's hand?" I asked.

"This is a form of respecting each other," she said. "It's part of being a good Muslim. Doing it every day makes sure you're purged of guilt and grudges. I do it from the bottom of my heart, not that I have necessarily done anything wrong. It's just a show of respect. My husband reciprocates, but in his own way."

And Manuel? What was the source of his happiness? Here's what he told me:

"When I was younger, I saw an ad for an electronics company in Texas looking for technicians who could speak English," he said. "But by the time I was 35, I'd lost my savings, my auto parts business, and my wife," he said. "I bought a gun and kept it in my bed, thinking I might use it on myself. Then one night God came to me and told me I had work to do." Manuel went on a diet and started to lose weight. With his mother's consent, he had a hole punched through his bedroom wall, installed double-wide glass doors to admit the world, and unleashed his knack for deal making. Today he receives up to 70 visitors a day—clients seeking to trade everything from blue jeans to Thompson helicopters, cousins and friends stopping by for a chat, or people seeking his business advice. He doesn't have to go looking for social interaction; it comes to him.

As I sat with him one evening, his cell phone rang and he lifted the tiny device to his ear. On the other end, a desperately overweight girl was searching for hope. "If I can turn my life around," he said tenderly, "you can too, dear." When he hung up, an old friend stopped by for a visit. Then another phone call. This time it was news that the website Manuel runs had crashed. In his smooth, unflappable voice, he troubleshot the problem with the webmaster. I sat back and watched. "Does this ever end?" I asked.

"If it did, I'd be dead," he said.

A year later, Manuel married Claudia. With her help, he has lost more than 500 pounds. Life has never been better.

These three individuals—a garbageman with time for his kids, a housewife surrounded by close friends, and a junk dealer on a personal mission of faith—share a common characteristic: They all consider themselves to be "very happy."

Thriving

According to the Gallup organization, "thriving" countries are those whose citizens think positively about their lives and report more happiness, enjoyment, interest, and respect. These countries also report significantly lower rates of health problems, sick days, stress, sadness, and anger.

More than that, they all believe that they will become even happier in the years to come. Like many people, they deal with challenges every day. They experience stress, periods of sadness, and grief. Life sometimes deals them a bad hand. They are, in many ways, not so different from the rest of us. Yet somehow they experience a sense of happiness greater than ours. Researchers have a term for this positive, optimistic condition: They call such people *thrivers*.

What's their secret?

During the past few decades, a small army of psychologists, social scientists, and scholars have asked the same question. Through rigorous experimentation and exhaustive surveys, they've given birth to a new science of happiness, focusing not only on defining the nature of human happiness, but also on discovering ways to improve our chances for personal well-being. Before we strike off around the world to learn the lessons of the world's happiness people, let's turn to some of the leading experts to understand the scientific fundamentals of the field:

Ed Diener, Ph.D., is Joseph R. Smiley Distinguished Professor of Psychology at the University of Illinois at Urbana-Champaign, and the author of *Happiness: Unlocking the Mysteries of Psychological Wealth.*

Sonja Lyubomirsky, Ph.D., is a professor of psychology at the University of California, Riverside, and the author of *The How of Happiness: A Scientific Approach to Getting the Life You Want.*

Ruut Veenhoven, Ph.D., is director of the World Database of Happiness and editor of the *Journal of Happiness Studies.*

Jim Harter, Ph.D., is chief scientist of workplace management and well-being for Gallup and coauthor of *12: The Elements of Great Managing* and *Wellbeing: The Five Essential Elements.*

Bruno S. Frey is a professor of economics at the University of Zurich and research director of CREMA (Center for Research in Economics, Management and the Arts). He is the author of *Happiness: A Revolution in Economics.*

Mihály Csíkszentmihályi is Distinguished Professor of Psychology and director of the Quality of Life Research Center at the Claremont Graduate University in Claremont, California.

In what follows, I've distilled ideas from their books as well as from my interviews with these experts and sorted their answers according to key questions. Here's what they told me.

WHAT IS HAPPINESS?

Mihály Csíkszentmihályi: As many a thinker since Aristotle has said, everything we do is ultimately aimed at experiencing happiness. We don't really want wealth, or health, or fame as such—we want these things because we hope they will make us happy. But happiness we seek not because it will get us something else, but for its own sake.

Sonja Lyubomirsky: I use the term "happiness" to refer to the experience of joy, contentment, or positive well-being, combined with a sense that one's life is good, meaningful, and worthwhile. However, most of us don't need a definition of happiness because we instinctively know whether we are happy or not.

Ed Diener: The word "happiness" means many things. It means positive emotions. It means life satisfaction. It means generally your life is going well. It means many different things in the different ways people use it. Everyone has this general idea. So I don't define happiness. I try to use these other, more exact terms, such as positive emotions, life satisfaction, marital satisfaction.

HOW DO YOU MEASURE HAPPINESS?
Sonja Lyubomirsky: We let people define happiness for themselves. There's no happiness thermometer. No one else can tell you how happy you are. It's a subjective phenomenon. No one but you knows, or should tell you, how happy you truly are.

Jim Harter: We ask people to rate the quality of their overall life today on a 0-10 ladder of life developed by Hadley Cantril of Princeton, and what they think it will be in the next five years—to tap into their "reflecting" self. The good news is that most people have a more positive view of the future than the present . . . maybe this keeps us striving for something better. We use responses to questions to categorize people as "thriving," "struggling," or "suffering." We also ask people to recall their experiences from the previous day. This allows us to tap into the "experiencing" self or how much positive and negative emotions and experiences people have on a typical day. These are both important aspects of well-being . . . the evaluating self and the experiencing self.

Ruut Veenhoven: In my definition, happiness is how much one likes the life one lives. So if people say they are happy they are happy, unless they are lying.

Ed Diener: The key is that each person is making the evaluation of his or her life—not an expert's, philosopher's, or somebody else. Thus, the person herself or himself is the expert: Is my life going well, according to the standards that I choose to use?

DO THE SAME THINGS MAKE EVERYONE HAPPY?

Sonja Lyubomirsky: There are many faces of happiness. The face of happiness may be someone who is intensely curious and enthusiastic about learning; it may be someone who is engrossed in plans for his next five years; it may be someone who can distinguish between the things that matter and the things that don't; it may be someone who looks forward each night to reading to her child. Some happy people may look outwardly cheerful or transparently serene, and others are simply busy. In other words, we all have the potential to be happy, each in our own way.

Ed Diener: Some things about happiness are universal. If everyone hates you, nobody respects you or supports you, that makes you unhappy, no matter who you are. But other things are unique. They depend on your personality. For example, I love analyzing data. Most people don't. They'd rather read a book, see a movie, or gossip. The evidence is strong that social relationships are now a basic need. The other things we talk about in terms of happiness are a little more abstract, like making progress toward your goals and values, and having purpose and meaning.

DO WE HAVE ANY CONTROL OVER OUR HAPPINESS?

Sonja Lyubomirsky: On average, 50 percent of individual differences in happiness is influenced by our genetic makeup, 10 percent is influenced by our life circumstances, and 40 percent is influenced by how we think and act every day. Research has shown that each of us is born with a kind of happiness "set point," a natural predisposition for happiness that we carry throughout our lives. But that doesn't mean your happiness *level* cannot be changed. We can rise above our happiness set points, just as we can rise above our set points for weight or cholesterol. Genuinely happy people do not just sit around being content. They make things happen. They pursue new understandings, seek new achievements, and control their thoughts and feelings. We can also learn from others. If an unhappy person wants to experience interest, enthusiasm, contentment, peace, and joy, he or she can make it happen by learning the habits of a happy person.

WHAT ARE THE MOST IMPORTANT FACTORS CONTRIBUTING TO HAPPINESS?

Sonja Lyubomirsky: We tend to look for happiness in the wrong places. What we believe would make a huge difference in our lives actually, according to scientific research, makes only a small difference, while we overlook the true sources of personal happiness and well-being. Many of us think that moving into a bigger house, securing a promotion or pay raise, or flying first class will boost our happiness. But such pleasures are fleeting, leaving us no happier than we were before. The true keys to happiness lie in changing the way we think and behave, seeking out experiences such as savoring a beautiful moment and taking a picture of it, thanking a friend, writing a gratitude journal, or performing random acts of kindness. Such habits add up to create an upward spiral that boosts happiness.

Jim Harter: When we considered factors that explain both life evaluations and daily experiences, we found five areas that individuals can act on: career, social, financial, physical, and community. Career well-being is more than just having a job and it is relevant for people in all different life stages and situations . . . students, people who work in the home, people who are retired, self-subsistence farmers, and people in traditional work settings. It's really what you do with your life, how you spend your time, whether it is enjoyable and meaningful.

The Truth About Happiness

Ed Diener: Here's what I would say to an auditorium of average people from Iowa (or wherever), if they asked me how to increase one's happiness: We can't control our genes, so why worry about that? We can control our behavior and our thinking, so that's what we focus on. It's not a scientific argument. It's a practical argument. Some of the most powerful things we can do involve our relationships with others.

Mihály Csíkszentmihályi: If one wants to improve the quality of everyday life, happiness may be the wrong place to start. Other feelings are much more influenced by what one does, who one is with, or the place one happens to be. These moods are more amenable to direct change, and because they are also connected to how happy we feel, in the long run they might lift our average level of happiness. For instance, how active, strong, and alert we feel depends a lot on what we do—these feelings become more intense when we are involved with a difficult task, and they get more attenuated when we fail at what we do, or when we don't try to do anything. The quality of life does not depend on happiness alone, but also on what one does to be happy. If one fails to develop goals that give meaning to one's existence, if one does not use the mind to its fullest, then good feelings fulfill just a fraction of the potential we possess. True happiness involves the pursuit of worthy goals. Without dreams, without risks, only a trivial semblance of living can be achieved.

CAN MONEY BUY HAPPINESS?

Sonja Lyubomirsky: The truth is that money *does* make us happy. But our misunderstanding, as one happiness researcher eloquently explains, is that "we think money will bring lots of happiness for a long time, and actually it brings a little happiness for a short time." Being wealthy has its advantages, of course. But it doesn't make us dramatically happier, she explains. The richest Americans, those earning more than ten million dollars annually, report levels of personal happiness only slightly greater than the office staffs and blue-collar workers they employ. The reason may be that wealthy people are preoccupied with staying wealthy. Meanwhile, in our effortful pursuit of such dead ends to pleasure, we end up ignoring other, more effective routes to well-being.

Ed Diener: Yes, money buys happiness, but there are important exceptions. Money is more than a fixed amount of legal tender. Wealth is, in part, also about your desires. Being satisfied with your paycheck, just like being satisfied with your life, is about your point of view. Studies have shown that an individual's income is a poor predictor of their happiness. Some people with a lot of money could not meet their desires, and others with little money were able to do so. Materialistic people, that is, are seldom the happiest people because they want too much. It is generally good for your happiness to *have* money, but toxic to your happiness to *want* money too much.

Bruno Frey: People make a mistake when it comes to predicting how much money will make them happy. Consider the individual who chooses a job with more income but a longer commute. If you get an increase in income, two-thirds to three-quarters of the happiness from that increase wears out in one year, because you get accustomed to a higher income level very quickly. But you never get used to a long commute.

Mihály Csíkszentmihályi: Material well-being is attractive and relatively easy to attain, but there's a point of diminishing returns. Kids that value material goals beyond a certain point end up not having many friends. They become selfish and more depressed. You can't pile up more things and expect an increase in well-being. The same thing holds true for society in general. There is only a very weak relationship between finances and satisfaction with life; billionaires in America are only infinitesimally happier than those with average incomes. One conclusion that the findings seem to justify is that beyond the threshold of poverty, additional resources do not appreciably improve the chances of being happy.

IS HAPPINESS CONTAGIOUS?

Sonja Lyubomirsky: Surrounding yourself with people who are happy is going to make you happier. Conversely, if you're married to a negative person, it's going to take a toll on you. The problem is that we adapt: We really have to work to appreciate what we have.

Ed Diener: It's certainly true that if you're around somebody that's giving you many compliments, you start giving people compliments yourself. If you're around people who are more positive in general, you get more positive. On the other hand, when you're unhappy and you're bitching all the time, you're not just affecting yourself, you're affecting other people, too, and you're also teaching them about how to act or not act.

IS HAPPINESS OVERRATED?

Ed Diener: We actually think it's underrated, rather than overrated. We think the reason everybody wants to be happy is because it's pleasant. It just feels good. We're saying, it's not just that. If you're happy, you function better. You're more sociable. You're a better citizen. You do volunteer work. You're healthier. All these things. Conversely, if you look at really unhappy people, angry and depressed people, they don't normally function well. Angry people are disruptive in group work. Depressed people, they're withdrawn, they have no energy. Nothing sounds good to them.

Unhappy Places

According to World Values Surveys from 1995 to 2007, the 10 unhappiest places on Earth are:
1. Zimbabwe, 2. Armenia, 3. Moldova, 4. Belarus, 5. Ukraine, 6. Albania, 7. Iraq, 8. Bulgaria, 9. Georgia, 10. Russia.

Sonja Lyubomirsky: A recent review of all the available literature has revealed that happiness does indeed have numerous positive by-products, which appear to benefit not only individuals, but families, communities, and the society at large. The benefits of happiness include higher income and superior work outcomes (e.g., greater productivity and higher quality of work); larger social rewards (e.g., more satisfying and longer marriages, more friends, stronger social support, and richer social interactions); more activity, energy, and flow; better physical health (e.g., a bolstered immune system, lowered stress levels, and less pain); and even longer life. The literature, my colleagues and I have found, also suggests that happy individuals are more creative, helpful, charitable, and self-confident; have better self-control; and show greater self-regulatory and coping abilities.

HAPPINESS BLUE ZONES

How can you benefit from the insights of these researchers and thrive in your daily life? The answer goes back to the quiz you took at the beginning of this chapter. As the stories about the garbageman, housewife, and bedridden wheeler-dealer demonstrate, happiness comes in many shapes and sizes. Although we might think we know what we need to be happy, such as physical beauty, financial success, or the recognition of our peers, the scientific evidence points in a different direction. The true sources of happiness, the experts say, are deeper patterns of behavior and thinking in our lives—patterns that we can adjust if we just put our minds to it.

Fortunately, we don't have to start this process of change from scratch. As we'll see in the chapters that follow, scientists have already identified places around the world where people today are experiencing levels of happiness and well-being that are probably higher than yours or mine. All we have to do is figure out how they do it, and then adapt their lessons to fit our lives.

In pursuit of this quest, the National Geographic Society sent me around the world to visit four of the happiest regions on three continents to see if I could find common denominators—a common recipe for human happiness. In each place I talked to writers, economists, social scientists, demographers, physiologists, anthropologists, a prime minister, and ordinary people to piece together the local formula for happiness. I examined which government policies seemed to yield the greatest well-being, which cultural norms encouraged the most happiness, and which personal habits and environmental factors favored the greatest life satisfaction. I used a science-based approach to probe the one sure source of knowledge about happiness: the people who are verifiably experiencing it. In the chapters that follow, you may be surprised by what people told me. You might find their stories of happiness hard to believe, especially when they spring from conditions that are difficult or challenging. But in the end I think you'll discover that these stories will reveal new ways of thinking, and that the lessons they offer can help you get more joy out of each day—and ultimately set up your life so that true, authentic, and lasting happiness can ensue.

Measuring Happiness

A number of polls measure happiness on a world scale. Here are a few of the most significant polls and what they address:

World Database of Happiness
Started in 1984, this collection of thousands of scientific research reports on happiness from around the world, compiled by Ruut Veenhoven at Erasmus University in Rotterdam, examines the subjective enjoyment of life, including feelings correlated with happiness, and how nations around the world compare with one another in terms of happiness levels.

World Values Survey
This worldwide network of social scientists has conducted surveys in 97 nations since 1981. Conducted in five waves, in collaboration with the European Values Study, the surveys assess the impact of changing values on social and political life.

Gallup World Poll—This poll, which synthesizes survey information from 155 countries, uses Gallup's global information gathering resources to identify the strengths and challenges faced by different countries and regions. Subjects were asked questions about economic conditions, government and business, health care and well-being, infrastructure and education, and life satisfaction.

Latinobarómetro—This public opinion survey is conducted annually in 18 Latin American countries with more than 400 million people and measures public opinion, attitudes, and behaviors on topics including trade, democracy, trust in institutions, and other topical issues pertaining to Latin American countries.

Eurobarometer—Conducted by the Public Opinion Analysis sector of the European Commission, the Eurobarometer has measured public perception of quality of life in various European cities.

CHAPTER TWO

Denmark:
The World's Happiness All-Stars

Kenneth and Lene Zibrandtsen play cards with their daughter, Astrid, on a candlelit evening in Copenhagen, embodying the Danish concept of hygge—"*the art of relaxing in a warm and cozy environment.*" PHOTO BY DAVID McLAIN/AURORA

Denmark:
The World's Happiness All-Stars

You can almost always learn something about a city by turning your nose skyward and taking in a breath. I'll never forget my first whiff of the diesel fumes in Lima, Peru. Or Seoul's relentless garlic breath. Or the aroma of cloves in Lamu, Kenya. Or the smell of human sweat in Lagos, Nigeria. But my first impression of Copenhagen was a puzzle. As far as I could tell, this city of more than a million people had no odor at all—or at most a hint of salt water from the nearby Baltic Sea.

"We try very hard to smell of nothing," my friend Anders Weber explained. "No one wants to stand out."

It was a warm afternoon, and the two of us were pedaling side by side down Copenhagen's cobblestone streets. Anders, a 29-year-old journalist, had alert blue eyes, fuzzy blond hair, and a pale complexion. On most mornings, his baritone voice could be heard on one of Denmark's most popular radio news programs, which he helped to produce. Lately, after work, he'd been acting as my guide, showing me around the city and helping to set up interviews.

We'd ditched our rental car the day before in favor of a pair of Mary Poppins-esque bicycles that now had become our research vehicles. My plan was to meet the people of Copenhagen up close and perhaps to witness some of Denmark's fabled happiness. As one study after another has shown, the people of this small Scandinavian nation consistently report levels of happiness and well-being near the very top of the scale, making them some of the world's happiness all-stars. What is it about their way of life that generates these positive feelings? And how is their sense of happiness different from those of people in other parts of the world? What is the Danish formula for happiness?

Along with a third of the population in Copenhagen, Anders can bike practically anywhere he needs to go. Here, unlike most parts of the world, bicyclists occupy the top of the food chain. Wide, double bike lanes, right-of-way priority, a healthy disdain for pollution, and a 900-year-old street grid designed for foot traffic give two-wheelers in the city a pronounced advantage over their four-wheeled counterparts. Bicyclists cruise side by side and hold conversations. Slow traffic stays to the right, while the Lycra-clad set whizzes by in the left lane. You see people chatting on their cell phones while riding. In fact, cycling here has achieved not only acceptance, but also a kind of hipness. Men on bikes wear suits and ties and carry their briefcases in high-fashion handlebar baskets. Women pedal in skirts and high heels. Because cycling is cool and easy, people here don't mind doing it. In fact, commuters in Copenhagen cycle more than a million kilometers *per day,* a routine that helps explain why Danes tend to be trimmer than their English, German, and Swedish neighbors.

As we pedaled through the waterfront Nyhavn district, Anders and I followed the routes of historic canals, flanked on one side by café-lined streets and on the other by buildings painted crimson, baby blue, and gold. Farther on, crossing the town square, we saw street vendors selling smoked herring (instead of snow cones and wieners like we have in Minnesota) from wagons on the zigzag brick pavement. In the heart of the city, we rumbled over centuries-old cobblestones on streets with gargling names like Lille Kirkestræde or Snaregade. Then, as we left the older part of town, we saw modern Danish architecture come to life in places like the Sluseholmen housing development, whose blocky white buildings clearly were designed by an architect who had been

Denmark Facts

Region: Northern Europe

Location: On a peninsula north of Germany bordered by the Baltic Sea and the North Sea

Population: 5.5 million people

obsessed with Legos as a kid, and the city's concert hall, which lights up at night like an iridescent cobalt blue cube.

As a cyclist, I've always regarded stoplights as more of a suggestion than a command—and then only when cross traffic is menacing. Not the Danes. At every crosswalk we passed, people dutifully waited for the green with their hands at their sides or buried in their pockets—including cyclists.

"Do Danes always do that?" I asked Anders.

"Of course," he replied. "It could be two in the morning, without even the hope of a passing car, and we'll wait for the light."

Something else I noticed during our tour: Despite Denmark's reputation as one of the happiest places on Earth, few of the ordinary citizens we passed seemed particularly cheerful. In fact, most pedestrians in Copenhagen struck me as reserved or even sullen. They kept to themselves as they walked down the streets. Like people in any big city, they appeared to be in a big hurry, and they avoided eye contact with those around them. This reminded me of Denmark's other reputation as a place with long winters, brooding intellectuals, and a troubling suicide rate. An outgoing Dane, as one joke puts it, is the guy who looks down at your shoes instead of his own. ("I'm shocked to hear we're a happy lot," a well-known comedian had told me. "Maybe Danes go home and act happy in their kitchens.") How did the serious side of their personalities fit into the happiness formula? Was I reading too much into casual observations? Or was this darkness another clue to understanding the Danish character?

The contradictions were intriguing. In survey after survey, Danes consistently outpace the rest of the world not only for the way they *experience* happiness, but also for their tendency to recognize their happiness when asked to *evaluate* their lives. To put it differently, the Danish people authentically *thrive*. But how does that sit with their sometimes gloomy outlook?

Questions like these were piling up in my mind as Anders and I ducked down Copenhagen's narrow streets. On one corner, I caught the eye of a friendly-looking young woman with a bowl haircut and a tie-dye T-shirt, and I waved as I rode by. She abruptly looked away.

"I wouldn't do that if I were you," cautioned Anders, pedaling next to me.

"Why not?" I asked.

"You'll stand out," he said.

"Can't I smile, at least?"

"I wouldn't do that either. It makes people uncomfortable."

"What if I gave them a big smile *and* waved?"

"Well, I don't know," Anders said gravely. "They'd probably call the police."

THE FIRST PIECES OF THE PUZZLE

As I was about to discover, getting to the bottom of a place's formula for happiness is like piecing together a puzzle. You pick up a fact here, a figure there, and once enough pieces are in place, the whole picture comes into view. One of the first experts I consulted in Denmark was Peter Gundelach, a sociologist from the University of Copenhagen, who recently had administered the European Values Survey in his country. A tall man with rimless glasses and a fringe of gray hair on a bald dome, Gundelach welcomed me to his office in a 150-year-old gray-brick building at the university. Eager to hear his insights, I starting peppering him with a string of why-are-Danes-so-happy questions. But he held up a finger to slow me down.

"You must remember," he said, "I'm not a psychologist. I conduct surveys of entire populations. I deal in averages."

Here's how his surveys work, he told me. Researchers start with 1,500 randomly selected names and addresses from the Danish census bureau. To each person they send a letter requesting an interview. For statistical purposes, he explained, 1,500 names are more than enough to get an accurate picture of Danish attitudes. "Imagine a swimming pool filled with five million black and white marbles," he said. "If you randomly pick 1,500 of them and discover that 39 percent are black and 61 percent are white, you can safely assume that the same ratio holds true for the entire pool, give or take a couple of percent."

About half of the recipients responded to the letter and agreed to a one-hour meeting, during which an interviewer asked 100 or so questions. Only three of these questions addressed happiness head-on, and they were all variations of the following: "Taking all things together, would you say you are 1) very happy, 2) quite happy, 3) not very happy, or 4) not at all happy?" The power of these surveys, Gundelach said, came not just from each individual's ranking of his or her level of happiness, but also from how the individual *corre-lated* that ranking to other aspects of his or her life. Such data, in the hands of statisticians, revealed which behaviors were most likely to be present in people who reported being happy.

Before telling me what his study revealed, though, Gundelach took a moment to give me some perspective. With a population of five and a half million, he reminded me, Denmark is one of the world's wealthier nations per capita. Danes spend relatively more money on their children and seniors than any other people. Lifelong health care is a Danish birthright. Education is free, and university students are *paid* to go to school. Doctor visits, x-rays, and surgeries are all covered by the state. If you have difficulty conceiving a baby, the government will pay for fertility treatments. And while it won't pay for your breast implants, it will cover the cleanup costs if the silicone springs a leak. If you're out of work (which is unlikely—unemployment is around four percent), the government will pay you to look for a job.

Other Happy Places

According to Ruut Veenhoven's World Database of Happiness, the happiest countries in the world are: 1. Costa Rica, 2. Denmark, 3. Iceland, 4. Switzerland, 5. Finland, 6. Mexico, 7. Norway, 8. Canada, 9. Panama, and 10. Sweden. The United States is ranked 20th in this survey.

"Denmark is a high-functioning country," said Gundelach, summing it up. "It's stable and safe. Your kids can play on the streets. You have this feeling that not very many things can go wrong. But if they do, there is someone to take care of you."

"But then again, you pay for it, don't you?" I said. Anyone making more than the equivalent of about $70,000 a year will part with 60 percent of it through taxes.

"Yes, but we see from the surveys that most people here are satisfied with the trade-off," Gundelach replied. Although Danes might grumble about high taxes, they approve of the results: a society with an extremely low disparity between rich and poor. As a popular slogan puts it, Denmark is a country "where few have too much and even fewer have too little."

Turning to the survey results, he said, we now know in some detail what makes people in Denmark happy. According to his research, the happiest Danes were most likely to:

- live around people they could trust
- live in a city (rather than in the country)
- feel like their opinions were heard
- live in a place with people of equal status
- feel secure
- be middle-aged
- be married or in a committed relationship

None of these factors by themselves guarantee happiness, Gundelach was quick to point out. His research on marriage, for example, suggests that, although married people were twice as likely to be happy as unmarried people, they were also more likely to be happy in the first place. But as I looked at his list, the factors seemed to be key building blocks for a happy society. I noticed that neither wealth nor status was in the mix of top values.

"So," I pressed, "what actually causes happiness here?"

"To begin with, no one has ever come up with an elegant definition of happiness," said Gundelach, hedging. "You can always be a little bit more happy, so there is no limit to the term. You can be satisfied—content with the difference between what you want and what you get." Then he paused to gather his thoughts. Exuding a patient, Scandinavian goodness, he seemed to sense that his answer had veered from my question. "I'm sorry," he said. "We can only measure what people say. It takes a lot of questions, and then a lot of math, to begin to figure out what we really feel and how that connects to happiness."

"So have you figured it out?" I asked.

"Well, Denmark is homogenous," he replied. "We share a common background. We look similar. We like the same food. We rally around the same flag—which is the oldest one in the world. So when the government asks us to make a sacrifice and pay 70 percent of our salary in taxes, we know it is for someone who is like us." He looked over at me and switched gears. "One of the reasons we think Danes are very happy is because they are very satisfied with their lives. Which means that life is very good here—or that Danes have very low expectations."

I understood what he meant about low expectations. Ask a Dane how he is, and he'll invariably answer *"Det kunne være være"*—"It could be worse"—a response that clearly doesn't focus on the wonderful things the day may have in store. But what does that mean for the rest of us? What lesson does it teach about achieving happiness in our own lives? It would be hard to imagine telling a Wall Street broker to cultivate low expectations, for example. So I kept on pushing.

"Anything else explain Danish happiness?" I asked.

"We don't really know," he said finally.

I shuffled my papers and waited for more. He looked away as the room filled with palpable unease.

"All right, I'll tell you what I think," he said at last, and lightly slapped the desk—a gesture of frustration by a numbers man who is uncomfortable straying too far from a spreadsheet. "I believe a lot of it goes back to the period after 1864, after we lost 25 percent of our territory to the Germans in the Schleswig-Holstein War. We had to abandon our ambitions to be a superpower. This is when our country began to change. Enlightenment came early here."

By enlightenment, he meant that Danes had learned the wisdom of turning their resources inward and focusing them on education, social institutions, and national pride. Gundelach went on to explain that Denmark's defeat gave rise to a populist educational movement. It was started by a poet, pastor, and hymn writer named Nikolai Grundtvig, who believed that, since everyone experiences emotions with equal quality and intensity, everyone is essentially equal. Education, he believed, should focus on asking the question "Who are you?" rather than "What can you do?" (Grundtvig once said, "A doctor may know more than a peasant, but a peasant and a doctor know more together.") This vision found expression in the founding of the *Folkehoejskoler,* or Danish folk high schools. These schools had no rules or exams—strictures that "deaden the soul," Grundtvig warned—but offered classes that prepared students for society and for participation in the arts. They promoted a spirit of freedom, equality, and disciplined creativity. The idea—for the first time in human history, Gundelach said— was to give peasants and other poor people a chance to appreciate the arts, to enjoy a poem, or to delight in a Mozart sonata.

For the next two hours, Gundelach developed this argument and began to tie it more closely to a national feeling of happiness. He said the folk school movement gave Danes the confidence they needed to rebuild—and the conviction that everyone needed to have a role in that rebuilding. It taught them to cooperate and to compromise, thus giving Denmark a head start in the practice of democracy. The schools spawned cooperatives, which led to Danish farm prosperity, he said. Among other accomplishments, the cooperatives standardized butter (made possible by centrifuges invented in the folk schools) and produced high-quality bacon. This emphasis upon consistent quality, a major innovation in the 19th century, helped to launch Denmark into the high-end economic niche for which the nation is still known today.

The cooperatives also gave rise to countless associations, which in many ways have defined Danish social life. Today 95 percent of Danes belong to one association or another—everything from labor unions to clubs for cold-water swimmers. For a people not known for being outgoing, these institutionalized social networks have been crucial in keeping Danes connected to one another. And this has boosted their level of happiness.

"But remember," Gundelach warned, "this is just me talking."

Perhaps, I thought, but he was making good sense. If you look at the results of all the surveys from 146 countries, you find that people who live in advanced democracies with strong social interaction tend to be happiest. But the idea of developing an individual's artistic ability as a means to create social harmony came as a revelation to me—as something uniquely Danish.

THE SUICIDE MYTH

As we got deeper into our research, Anders and I developed a daily routine. Every afternoon I'd meet him at his apartment,

Pedal Power

In Copenhagen, one of the happiest cities in the world, 32% of workers bike to work daily. Even in rainy weather, 60% will still cycle, and 66% will continue to ride their bikes during the winter months.

a small place that looks like Van Gogh's "Bedroom at Arles" with its wood-planked floors, simple furniture, and framed landscapes on the walls. Then, sitting at his wooden table, we'd go over a list of people to interview. My initial conversation with Gundelach had sparked several interesting ideas in my mind, and I was eager to follow up on them. For example, I had my doubts about how well Danes accept the 60 percent tax rate. Are they really happy paying two-thirds of their income to the government—no matter how good the services? What does that do to their motivation? Do people really work? I also wanted to dig deeper into a few of the unique qualities of Danish culture—the way kids are raised, for one—and how these qualities relate to Danish happiness. Where does their sense of trust in one another come from? Or their penchant for "being heard"?

We decided to pay a visit to Rolf Jensen, who was then executive director of the Copenhagen Institute for Future Studies. A short man of about 60 with a pleasant disposition and red-rimmed glasses, Jensen had done a lot of thinking about how shifting values change the way we live and do business. His international best seller, *The Dream Society,* had correctly predicted that marketers would soon need to differentiate brands by creating stories about them to explain what they are and what they stand for (think Patagonia or Whole Foods). By the time we left Anders's apartment for our meeting, we were running a little late. Anders called ahead to let Jensen know.

"I suggest to you that you just relax and get here when you get here," Jensen said calmly. I loved his attitude, which reminded me of a Danish workplace study showing that, for most people, running late generated more stress than the workload involved. So Anders and I stopped for a quick lunch and showed up half an hour late. "I can offer you coffee, water, or a compromise: water and coffee," Jensen joked as he greeted us. He didn't even mention the time.

Jensen had taken a close look at the World Values Survey that ranks Denmark near the top for happiness, and he'd concluded that the two most important factors are the nation's commitments to tolerance and equality. Consider, for example, the way that Danes answered the following survey question: "Do you think that there is something good or right about all religions?" In general, Danes said yes. A second question asked if children should be raised to be good citizens or to be self-reliant. To that question most Danes answered "self-reliant." Status seekers are frowned upon in Denmark, Jensen said. "If you ride a taxi, you sit in the front seat. If you buy a new BMW, people will look down on you and wonder if you have some problems with your masculinity."

When I asked him where this tradition of enforced modesty came from, he told me a story. In the 1930s, he said, a Danish-Norwegian writer by the name of Aksel Sandemose wrote a book called *A Fugitive Crosses His Tracks,* which describes life in the fictional small town of Jante. In this town, people live by a set of informal rules such as "Don't think you're smarter than us" or "Don't think you can teach us anything." The Jante law, as these rules came to be known, captured the small-town Scandinavian mentality insisting that no one is better than anyone else. "And if you think you are, you'll be cut down," Jensen said.

"So how does that contribute to Danish happiness?" I asked. It didn't seem very helpful.

"On the contrary," he said. "The surveys show very clearly that countries where people have roughly the same level of status are happier than those places where you have a few haves and many have-nots. In Denmark, we have the Jante law mentality to thank for that."

When I asked about the long, dark winters in Denmark and the country's high rate of suicide, he countered that both are overblown. In recent years the nation's ranking for suicides had fallen from number one in the world to number fifteen. "Besides, Danes are a stoic people who report these things accurately," he pointed out. "If Daddy hangs himself, it's reported straightforwardly as a suicide. In Italy, if Father hangs himself, it would bring shame on the family and therefore might be reported as an accidental death." As for the dreary months of winter, he acknowledged that darkness lasts as long as 17 hours a day in Denmark. But Danes compensate for this by creating warm, candlelit environments to share with the company of friends. They even have a word for this, he said: *hygge,* which translates into a blend of "coziness" and "tranquillity."

THE PROBLEM WITH HARD WORK

Our next stop was with Tøger Seidenfaden, editor in chief of *Politiken,* Copenhagen's left-leaning daily newspaper. I'd recently seen him on *60 Minutes,* on which he discussed cartoons, published in Danish papers, that lampooned the prophet Muhammad. I'd been impressed by his Yale degree and insights into the Danish character. I figured he must have some thoughts about happiness.

The newspaper is located in a castle-like brick building overlooking a busy downtown square. As I waited in his corner office, I noticed a stern portrait of Viggo Hørup, the newspaper's founder, staring down from the wall. Then the door swung open and in whirled Seidenfaden, wearing a coffee-stained white shirt and leather sandals. A wandering forelock dangled over his forehead from an otherwise thinning head of blond hair.

"I didn't believe you," he said by way of greeting me as he shook my hand. He was referring to a note I'd sent to him about how Danes are some of the world's happiest people. "But since you contacted me, I've done some research on Danish happiness, and I have some theories for you." A recent report, he said, had noted that Danes eat more sweets than any other people in Europe. "Danes love to eat," he confirmed, his roundish figure suggesting that he was speaking from personal experience. "There's a saying in this country, 'If a man comes at you carrying a knife, you can be pretty sure he has a fork in the other hand.'"

Turning serious, he raised the issue of Danes' wanting to be heard, which Gundelach also had cited from his research. "From the time that Danes are in kindergarten, they expect to have a say in things," Seidenfaden said. "They vote for what to have for dinner, where the family goes on vacation, even for how to be punished if they have misbehaved. The other side of that equation is responsibility. They're expected to help with dinner and to behave. When we grow up, we have a similar relationship with the government. We expect the government to hear us and to take care of us. But on the other hand, we also expect to obey the rules."

One result of this, Seidenfaden explained, is that consensus is very important to Danes. He said, "Each week we print some 700 letters to the editor, and all of them begin, 'A lot of us think that . . . ' It's in our DNA. And because we live in a place where we can live out our values. It might explain your happiness finding."

We'd been talking for more than 30 minutes. Since Seidenfaden ran one of Denmark's biggest newspapers, I figured he'd be extraordinarily busy, and I should try to wrap it up. But no. The subject of happiness interested him, and he wanted to keep talking. "Work gets itself done," he said. Then, picking up the theme, he said that Danish workers put in only 37 hours a week before going home to their families, hobbies, or clubs. They take an average of six weeks of vacation a year (as opposed to the American average of eight to sixteen days).

"I don't believe in the workaholic culture," Seidenfaden told me. "I work as little as possible, and go home most days by the mid-afternoon. I get a good night's sleep. I always take my seven weeks of vacation. And somehow I always get my work done."

"Isn't there a price for that?" I asked. Critics might argue that such liberal work policies result in low productivity.

"I don't believe that either," he shot back. "I lived in the United States long enough to know that people spend a lot of their workday checking their e-mails and chatting at the watercooler. Here in Denmark we're Protestant and puritanical. Our work is important to our identities. But we get it done and go home to our families and friends."

HAPPY TAXES

Following up on the subject of taxes and work, I decided to try next for an interview with a high-ranking government official. In contrast to Washington, where it might take weeks of negotiating with handlers and media officials to set up an interview with an American politician, it took only two brief phone calls. The next day, a Saturday, Anders and I headed to Humlebaek, a village north of Copenhagen where low thatched-roof cottages faced a slate gray sea. At one cottage, fronted by a white picket fence and a small garden of gladiolus, we knocked on the door. A big man with glasses, sandy brown hair, and a crimson and gold Minnesota Gophers sweatshirt tucked into blue jeans answered with an ebullient "Hello." This was Claus Hjort Frederiksen, at the time Denmark's labor minister, who was also acting prime minister while his colleague was abroad.

"Come on in," he said with a smile.

We ducked into a low-ceilinged, simply furnished living room originally built by 17th-century peasants. Frederiksen led us to a couch and sat us down. His wife came in and asked, "Claus, will you be wanting a cup of coffee?" Once more, I was reminded of Denmark's casual society.

Denmark: The World's Happiness All-Stars

When I told Frederiksen about the worldwide happiness studies, he was surprised to hear that Denmark consistently came out near the top. But if the surveys were correct, he said, it was probably a function of the nation's economic prosperity. Located at a geographical gateway between Scandinavia and the rest of Europe, Denmark has always enjoyed a trade advantage, he pointed out. "Most Danes speak a few languages, and we are good at a trade," he said. "We have a reputation for trust, so the world likes to do business with us. Trust acts as lubricant in the gears of business and makes it spin faster and more smoothly."

"Yes," I agreed, "but don't high taxes tend to slow those gears down?"

"Sometimes," he replied. "But Danes say they don't mind given the services they receive." By way of example, he pointed to what happens when Danes start a family. Because of Denmark's labor market policies, a father has a right to stay at home with the baby for almost a year. In addition to the parents' rights to receive benefits during periods of leave, a father employed in the public sector will enjoy a right of up to 14 weeks with full salary. "It's hard to complain when most of your basic needs are covered," he said.

When the time came for us to leave, I asked him about his sweatshirt. "You know I'm from Minnesota," I told him. "Did you wear that for me?"

"My kids tell me this is the fashion," he laughed. "I'm wearing it to be cool."

ROYAL INSIGHT

As I continued my research in Copenhagen, I became a commuter like everybody else. During the day I'd conduct interviews in the city. Then, each afternoon, I'd take a half-hour train ride to my temporary lodgings in the suburbs. Unlike everybody else, however, I was staying on the grounds of an 18th-century palace.

My home away from home was Ledreborg Palace, where I was the guest of a longtime friend, Remar Sutton. Though of relatively modest means—he was the *Washington Post*'s consumer columnist for years—Remar winters in the British Virgin Islands and spends his summers here in Denmark. He's a man who attracts a wide range of friends with a sweet Southern drawl and an addictive charm. On any given Tuesday night, one might find a billionaire, a Dutch surfer, a Kennedy or Eisenhower, and a West Indian farmer in his kitchen. Countess Silvia Munro and her husband, Jock, the owners of the palace, number among his pals. Several years ago they gave Remar a leasehold on a secluded 300-year-old cottage largely just to have him around. Remar built two tiny but stylish guest cottages and refurbished his own with art deco furniture from a thrift shop and some good art. He then optimized his grounds for outdoor summer entertainment. Rustic picnic tables along a low rock wall seat 48 people, 100 torches light the grounds at night, and the terraced gardens bloom from June to November. Two glass summerhouses in the garden serve as an outdoor sitting room and dining room, just feet from an inviting fire pit that seats 24 on large stones, sheltered from the wind by a crescent of giant oaks.

At the end of my first week there, Remar offered to turn one of these evenings into a "happiness party."

"Invite anyone you want," he said.

I invited Anders, Gundelach, and a number of the other people I'd interviewed. By 8:30 that night, with the sun heading down, guests started to arrive. Remar had lit the torches, which illuminated the gardens and picnic area, and had set picnic tables with glassware and tall candles before starting the grill. The goal was to have fun—and to thank my guests for their help—but I also knew that a number of these experts hadn't yet met one another. I fully expected more insights about happiness to flow with the conversation and wine.

His Royal Highness Prince Philippe de Bourbon-Parme walked over from his summer home with his wife and two sons—a trio of princes and a princess. The Bourbons, as with most of the cousins, are related to many of the royal families of Europe. Philippe is a direct descendant of France's Louis XIV and is the great-great-grandson of a Danish king. Silvia and Jock Munro arrived on horseback from the palace. His Highness Dimitri Romanoff, Prince of the House of Russia, also showed up.

At least ten young people—all cousins, virtually all a prince, princess, baron, count, or countess—arrived as well, many with young children and dogs in tow. This was an A-list of European royalty with every bit the pedigree of, say, Charles, the Prince of Wales. But this courtly gathering stood around wearing jeans, drinking beer, and nibbling from a cheese plate. It looked like a slightly upscale version of a Minnesota potluck, except the guy next to you eating a wiener might be the grandson of Czar Nicholas II (he was). Like everything else in Denmark, even royalty is modest and sensible.

Silvia and Jock Munro are handsome, middle-aged parents of four children whom they sent to public school. They loathe attention. In fact, Silvia relinquished one of her titles to protect her privacy. The couple's palace, with its priceless antiques, hundreds of paintings, and Versailles-like grounds, may suggest a life of leisure. But property taxes and the Danish work ethic keep the couple busy 50 hours a week. To maintain the place as a family home, Silvia and Jock rent out the vast outbuildings and separate dining halls for corporate events, and they sponsor concerts during the summer in their private park. Recently they turned a few hundred acres of pasture, framed with thousands of giant trees, into a golf course. Sixty years ago, hundreds of workers and palace staff helped run the estate. Now, 13 do the job, and most of these employees are foresters, groundsmen, and gamekeepers.

"I would have been much better off as a plumber," Jock once quipped to me.

John and Susan Donaldson, friends of Remar's, are similarly humble. John is a Scotsman raised in Tasmania. Susan Moody, his second wife, is a well-known British crime writer. When John's daughter, Mary, married Frederik, Crown Prince of Denmark, John and Susan became instant celebrities. Many Danes call John the Grandfather of All Danes, since his grandson is in line to become the king. You see John and Susan in royal portraits on postcards in every gift shop, and the tabloid press continually hounds them. Yet John, who wears boots and a Paul Bunyan beard, is a quiet and thoughtful math professor, and Susan, who looks like your favorite aunt, avoids the press at every turn.

The person who most stood out to me, though, was 19-year-old Prince Joseph de Bourbon-Parme, Philippe's youngest son. Joe is six feet three, blue-eyed, and built like a lumberjack. His smile is stunning, and he hugs friends and cousins alike when he greets them. At his age, other European royals would be forced into law or business schools to carry forth the family legacy and fortune. Not Joseph. He found his passion in woodwork. Joe was a carpenter's apprentice, and had two years left to finish his schooling.

"Why didn't you push your son into doing something, well, more regal?" I asked his father.

"Whatever for?" Philippe retorted with a smile. "I want him to be happy with what he does."

Remar, who is 68, and even in jeans and flip-flops still manages to project Southern charm, stood up and called for the group's attention with a fork tap on his wineglass.

"National Geographic has come to our little world to find the secret of happiness, and it is our duty to help," he said. He then posed the topic to his guests: "Let's tell Danny what it is about Danes that might explain why they are happier than everyone else."

"Well, I can tell you that they have a maddening obsession with consensus," began Jock, a Scotsman by birth, who had lived in Denmark for 25 years. "If you live in an apartment building, they will have a meeting to discuss what color to paint the walls and spend three hours deciding to paint it green, making sure everyone has a voice. And no statement is too ridiculous. Even if you say something really stupid, someone will respond, sincerely, by saying, 'Thank you for sharing.'"

"Yes, but that's what's important to Danes," added a sociologist who referred to a recent study showing that, in terms of work satisfaction, Danes who were happy in their work environment, even if they were paid less per hour, were more likely to stay at their jobs. The research suggests that Danes appreciated their work satisfaction more than their weekly paycheck. "For many of us, having a voice brings us more happiness than money does," he said.

"I think money and success are the secret to happiness. It's as simple as that," retorted Philippe Bourbon, a dead ringer for Prince Albert with his round, ruddy face; longish brown hair; full beard; and upturned mustache. "But then again," he said after a pause, "your neighbor's failure isn't bad either."

We moved on to dessert. The summer dusk descended as the sky muted from milky blue to a luminescent lavender. Remar tapped me on the shoulder and ushered me to the other end of the table where a lean, casually dressed woman sat quietly eating her cake. She seemed unfazed by the party's fuss and confusion. She was Countess Marie Holstein-Ledreborg, known affectionately as Aunt Marie, "the happiest person you'll meet in Denmark," Remar assured me.

At 87, Marie had largely shunned a lifetime of pomp and palace etiquette for the life of a photographer. She also has no fear. When seated next to a guest of Remar's who had just flown in by private jet, Marie turned to him and asked, "And how much of your fortune did you steal?"

I pulled up a chair next to Marie and told her that I was researching happiness. I asked if she might have some insight.

"I don't really think I can help you," she replied politely and looked away. But a few moments later she turned back to me with a thought. "You know, I was part of the Danish Resistance during World War II. The Nazis captured and imprisoned me. I didn't know if they were going to release me, take me to Germany, or kill me. They kept me like this for five weeks."

She fell silent again and stared blankly through her glasses.

"Getting over a difficult experience is a gift," she continued. "Then you know what life is worth. You don't always think about it, but you always carry it with you."

ON TO THE WORLD'S HAPPIEST PLACE

Taking stock of what I'd learned so far, the pieces of the Danish puzzle were starting to fall into place. The high taxes that I had initially been skeptical about apparently serve to nudge Danes away from pursuing material wealth to an excessive degree, while providing them with the kind of long-term satisfaction that comes from education, health care, and an economic safety net. The folk school tradition, meanwhile, imbued Danes with an appreciation of the arts, a populist sense of democracy, and a habit of joining clubs that keeps these Scandinavians from becoming socially isolated. Danish happiness, it seems, is also strongly linked to the trust that ordinary citizens feel for one another and to their sense that their feelings and opinions are adequately heard. Now I wanted to meet some of these ordinary people, talk to them, and find out how well these theories held up. So I went back to the databases and identified the region of Denmark that reported the highest levels of happiness. They pointed me to a surprising community on the Jutland Peninsula.

If you could distill all the wisdom from the 4,000 or so academic papers that have been written about happiness over the past decade and use it to design a place that would make the most people happy, it wouldn't be one where the streets are paved with gold, or one that has a magnificent view of the mountains or the sea. Little space would be used for luxury shops, country clubs, oversized houses, or other places that distinguish the wealthy from other classes. Instead, it would be a place with good schools, free health clinics, day care centers, and diverse places of worship dotting leafy urban neighborhoods. Bars, cafés, and social clubs would abound, and sidewalks would connect them. Nature—not suburbs—would surround a quiet yet culturally vibrant downtown. Citizens would be inclined to marry but free to divorce, trustworthy but not nosy, questioning of authority but not judgmental of their neighbors. Women would have engaging—but not all-consuming—jobs close to home. Few people would have too much, and fewer would have too little.

Welcome to the city of Århus. Here, people rate themselves on average as 8.5 out of a possible 10 on the happiness scale—among the highest in the world. Located a hundred miles west of Copenhagen, it's a region of sensible shoes, pickled herring, and 300,000 or so mostly fair-skinned Lutherans. During the long summer they picnic in the parks and stay late to drink wine under the midnight sun. During the long winter nights, they find their own brand of joy as they huddle around candle-light and sing songs to entertain one another. On any given day in Århus, you can join a club to play with model trains, to swim in subfreezing waters, or to train rabbits for jumping competi-tions. Hans Christian Andersen lived here for a while, as did St. Nicholas, who is buried in a quiet cemetery near a row of 16th-century houses. In size, arts, ostentation, and notoriety, Århus plays second fiddle to much bigger Copenhagen—but that makes it perfectly Danish. For this is a city in a country with a smug inferiority complex. "We are the most modest people on

Room to Breathe

The 5 least densely populated states in the U.S. (Alaska, Wyoming, Montana, North Dakota, and South Dakota) all made Gallup's list of the 10 least stressed states. People tend to be happier when they have room to stretch out. Densely populated Maryland is a noteworthy exception to this trend.

Earth," poet-scientist Piet Hein once said of Denmark, "and in that way are better than everyone else."

Downtown Århus sits like a giant amphitheater facing the sea that the Danes call the Kattegat, a body of water connecting the Baltic Sea with the North Sea. My home was a tiny room in the Cabin Hotel, where all the rooms are modeled after ship cabins (and bathrooms double as shower stalls). I frequently ate in bistros around the central square beneath the shadow of Århus Cathedral, with its 315-foot tower. From there it was a short walk to the office of the former mayor, a freckled brunette named Louise Gade, who'd been elected at the age of 29. When I stopped by for an interview one morning, a breakfast of fruit, bread, and coffee had been set for us. We talked about my hometown of Minneapolis, where she'd recently been for a conference, before turning to the subject of happiness. For the people of Århus, she said, the keys are small-town friendliness and ready access to nature.

"We're a city of 300,000, and yet you can walk to the sea or to the forest," she said. Their city is big enough to have a cosmopolitan museum and entertainment complex—Paul McCartney, Sting, and Depeche Mode have all given concerts there recently—yet small enough that residents still know one another by their first names. When asked what makes her happy (she rates her happiness as a 10), she told me about a hibiscus plant she was growing at home.

"I wake up in the morning and I see that flower, with the dew on its petals, and at the way it's folding out, and it makes me happy," she said. "It's important to focus on the things in the here and now, I think. In a month, the flower will be shriveled and you will miss its beauty if you don't make the effort to do it now. Your life, eventually, is the same way."

LEARNING THE ART OF LIVING

A few days later, I struck off by bike for Odder, a town about a dozen miles south of Århus. As I pedaled beyond the limits of the city, I came upon fruit stands set out by farmers to sell strawberries on the honor system. Next to their crated berries the farmers had left an open box with a sign posting the price, usually about two dollars a pint. Customers would take what they wanted and leave their money. One box, I noticed, held the equivalent of $20 in Danish kroner. Apparently no one was worried about anyone ripping off the berries and taking the money, too.

For me, this jogged a memory. In Århus I'd met a young economics professor named Christian Bjørnskov, who'd speculated that the trust Danes have for one another—partly based on a lack of corruption among public officials and a good legal system—was probably the most important factor contributing to their happiness. Danes scored highest for trust in the world, Bjørnskov told me. He traced this trust to the Vikings, who told stories of terrible things happening to people who didn't keep their word. He also credited the Protestant belief system that makes individuals responsible for their actions (no Catholic absolution here).

"It's just so much easier living in a place where you can trust one another," he'd said. "You don't have to lock your doors. Business can get done with a handshake and a lot fewer lawyers."

In the village of Beder, about halfway on my journey, I stopped at an old church. Inside (the door was unlocked, of course) it was cool and smelled pleasantly of old must and faded incense. A pipe organ dominated one end of the church; an elevated wooden pulpit and simple altar with an open Bible lay at the other. In between, a dozen rows of simple pews, flanked by candle stands, stood on an ancient stone floor. I imagined the lit candles, the warm and cozy *hygge* of Christmas Midnight Mass, and the congregation dressed in tweedy finery and singing sweet Grundtvig hymns.

For a moment, I felt envious of this culture of strong traditions and palpable history. In so much of the United States, everything seems fleeting and ephemeral. I thought of our holiday season, launched with Black Friday sales at the mall and concluded with a glut of unneeded gifts in a sea of discarded wrapping paper. By contrast, many Danes still sing around the Christmas tree, go to Midnight Mass in churches like this, and then, as a holiday treat, eat rice porridge with slivered almonds and cherry sauce.

Entering the village of Odder, I pedaled down the main street with buildings like gingerbread houses. I had come to see the legacy of the folk schools that had so shaped the Danish character. Now, after I'd spent a couple of weeks trying to put my finger on what explains Danish happiness, I kept coming back to Grundtvig's theory about these schools. I was increasingly convinced that the folk schools had helped create an environment that favored what psychologist Mihály Csíkszentmihályi calls "flow": an authentically happy state of engaged activity that supremely interests you, optimally challenges you, and occasionally makes time melt away. Though these institutions have continued to evolve during the past century—now they cater to college students in search of a life path and older people seeking intellectual enrichment—they still preserve Grundtvig's vision of a liberal arts education in an atmosphere of active participation. About 60,000 Danes a year go through a course at one of the country's 74 folk schools.

I met Jørgen Carlsen, the headmaster of the local folk school, in his cluttered office in the attic of an old building. A poster on his office door showed a stenciled portrait of him with a Jerry Garcia beard and glasses. The caption read, in Danish, "To Hell with Skills." A middle-aged family man, Carlsen described his job as a "calling"—part priest, part policeman, and part teacher. He taught classes until two o'clock, walked home for

Finding Flow

Psychologist Mihály Csíkszentmihályi describes "flow" as a state in which a person is fully immersed in what he or she is doing. This frequently occurs when a challenging task requires a high degree of skill, such as while playing an instrument, creating art, fixing a car, or while attempting any task that calls for a particular skill, talent, or passion.

lunch and a nap, and returned in the late afternoon for his administrative duties. Occasionally he'd stay late for school activities or attend the weekly meeting of the local water society. In the summer, he went to his second home by the sea.

"I think part of Danish happiness is that we're never more than 60 kilometers from the sea," he said. "That creates a sense that there are no obstacles for us and reinforces the freedom we Danes feel over our lives. We're free, by and large, to decide how we will use our time. We delight at the white nights when the sun sets at midnight, and we stay out late and drink wine in outdoor cafés. And even midwinter when, with a song and candles, we can create warmth even in the middle of a cold winter's night."

Students at Carlsen's school agree to attend morning assembly, all classes, and social events, and to participate actively in songs and poetry. Classes in the 12-week program, which are held mornings only, range from pottery to politics. Afternoons are free for independent study, socializing, and exercise in the countryside. Students come together for dinner, and at night the school offers workshops and theater.

"The idea is to give people an idea of the richness of life," Carlsen explained. "We believe that a rich person is not necessarily the one with a lot of money. It's the one who really has a lot to be grateful for: nature, the company of other people, the capacity to enjoy a good book, and an understanding of philosophy. The more things for which you develop a fondness, the richer the life you live. We're in the business of cultivating those fondnesses."

That was certainly the case with Michael Artmann, a 40-year-old man I met in Århus. Growing up in a working-class family, he'd never expected to make much of his life, he told me. His mother, a cleaning lady, had rarely pushed him to do well in school and, as a result, he had rarely tried. When he graduated, he was functionally illiterate. After trying a series of odd jobs, he got an apprenticeship as a metalworker and ended up on an oil rig in the North Sea. He fell in love with a more educated woman, a biologist, who had decided to become an artist. Then, in 1998, during a slump in the oil industry, he decided to take a year off.

"My life was work and drink," he admitted. "And then I enrolled in a folk school." I'd met Artmann at a community center called HUSET, a three-story former museum where people did carpentry, painted, and made jewelry. Michael was working part-time at the center as a volunteer pottery teacher. "The folk school changed everything for me," he said. "I took courses in ceramics and outdoor living and discovered that I have some real talents. At age 36, it even inspired me to learn to read." We were sitting across from each other at a pottery wheel. He looked both young and old, with crow's-feet and a creased forehead but also a full head of blond-tipped hair, an earring, and a tight-fitting T-shirt that read Big League.

"I decided that I wanted to be a schoolteacher and spent the next year learning," he continued. "All I did was sleep, eat, go to school, and study. I essentially crammed 12 years of education into 12 months. Now I have the fundamentals. I feel like I can breathe." He gestured outward from his chest. Red clay rimmed his fingernails. "I know how to use a computer, and I have just been accepted into the university college. Soon

I will be a teacher. I get about $900 a month to go to school, which doesn't pay for much. But it's enough for me to rent a small place, to buy food and school supplies."

"I don't get it," I said. "You make almost no money, you go to school full-time, yet you volunteer 30 hours a week here? Why?"

"Because I feel at home here, and I feel very satisfied that I can help," he replied. "For so many years, I've had nothing to offer except welding pipes. I started by taking classes and then throwing pots for my own personal enjoyment. Then people came to ask me for help. It was easy for me to do. I found I could make them happy with almost no effort. For the first time, I could make my own decision about where to work and, at the same time, make a difference."

HOW TO RAISE A FAMILY

It's 5:15 a.m. in August on the outskirts of Århus. I've just woken up on a futon on a floor of polished birch. Overhead is an elegant light fixture encased in a white origami starburst. In one corner I notice a stylish Bang & Olufsen stereo and a bean-bag chair in the shape of a lopsided cut diamond; in another corner is a lounge chair for reading. The room is long, flanked on both sides by floor-to-ceiling shelves, and capped on both ends with windows, into which the lavender light of morning sifts through gauzy curtains. The shelves contain artifacts of a life richly lived: books, a clarinet and sheet music, a stack of jazz albums, a model ship, a world atlas open to the page of a future vacation. Conspicuously missing are a clock and a TV—two enemies of a hobby, a musical instrument, or a good book.

Denmark: The World's Happiness All-Stars

A long table dominates the middle of the room. Several ad hoc workstations are set up: a laptop computer and ledger at one end of the table, and knitting needles, yarn, and the beginnings of a gray wool sweater at the other. In the middle, textbooks and notebooks lie open with pencils and pens. This is a Danish family room—or, as I would later come to think of it, a "destination" room—an ideal environment in which a family can thrive. A space like this, it occurred to me, clearly has its roots in Grundtvig's folk schools.

This is the home of Erik Kristiansen, who lives with his wife, Susan, their teenage daughters, Esther and Hannah, and their 13-year-old son, Peter. It's a small, four-room brick house. I'd met Erik the previous week at a downtown bookstore café. With his shaved head, muscular build, and angular features, Erik had a sort of David Beckman good looks. He was getting glances from a group of mothers who were chatting and drinking coffee next to us, having left their baby carriages parked outside (with babies) along a pedestrian mall—a regular practice among the trusting Danes. Erik was wearing a T-shirt and jeans, which struck me as odd at the time since he was coming from work. But his job calls for casual clothes. He works for a small business that takes employees into the forest to coach them how to be more productive. When I mentioned that I was in Århus looking into Danish happiness and hoping to shadow someone for a few days, he immediately agreed. "Well," he admitted, "I'm Danish, and I'm very happy."

When we arrived at his house that night, Susan was making salmon and potato salad in the kitchen. The kitchen was tight, with compact appliances—a stainless-steel stove, a washer and dryer stacked in the corner. Soccer schedules, notices of upcoming concerts, and a family picture hung on the walls. On an erasable board there was a cooking schedule that listed each family member's meal assignment. When we arrived, Hanna, the younger daughter, was directing her mother to marinate the fish and instructing her siblings to peel potatoes while she prepared an appetizer of olives, nuts, pickles, and bread. (Erik would later explain that this tight space was a training ground of sorts for reaching consensus, since it forced five people to constantly negotiate with one another.)

We ate dinner at a small kitchen table set with spoons fringed with fork-like prongs—a kind of spork. (In Denmark, everything seems carefully designed.) Votive candles flickered on the counter, while taller candles lit the table, to create the famously Danish warm, homey ambiance—*hygge*—that helps them endure their long, dark winters. Addressing no one in particular, I asked how they reacted to the notion that Århus could be one of the happiest places in the world.

"I smile," Erik replied. "I think it could be true, but we don't think about it. But when I think of it now, Århus is a not a big city but big enough to give you the opportunity to go to sporting events and concerts. We're close to nature. If you're in the center of town, you can bike in any direction and you're in nature within ten minutes. And there's not a lot of pretense here. Instead of spending our money on a car or clothes, we spend it on going to Greece, or camping in the forest."

"We don't like too much authority," Susan added. "But we trust the policemen and the government. And in turn, we obey rules that society sets for us not because we think we have to, but because it's part of a social contract. From a very early age, we're taught to have a voice. My children not only decide what we eat, but by the time they are six, they have had an equal voice in where we take our family vacation and how we budget for household expenses. They call their teachers by their first names."

"Is that true?" I asked, looking at Peter.

"Yes," he replied. "I decided what you're eating tonight."

After dinner, the kids didn't disappear to watch TV (the family has only a single small set) or to play video games. Instead, as their summer after-dinner ritual dictates, they moved out to the backyard, where Peter built a fire in a small pit and the conversation continued. "This is the time my family usually talks about their day," Erik told me. "We're away from the food and confusion and the daily schedules. This is the time we connect." I looked at 13-year-old Peter.

"Wouldn't you rather be watching TV?" I asked.

"Actually, no," he said.

This family seemed almost too perfect. But they were just being Danish.

THE PARAGON OF DANISH HAPPINESS

Before leaving Denmark, I met one more individual whose story has stuck with me. At first glance, Jørn Munk Hemmingsen might not seem to be an ideal candidate for happiness. A former attorney in a high-powered Copenhagen firm, he sat down one afternoon ten years ago and wrote a letter of resignation to his partners. He didn't tell his wife what he was going to do, because he knew that if he did, the two of them would discuss the idea for months, and he'd probably never go through with it. In the letter, he acknowledged his 18 productive years at the firm and thanked his partners for their integrity and friendship. He said he wasn't unhappy with the working conditions and that he had been paid more than enough money. "Nevertheless, as of midnight tonight," he wrote, "I will be resigning my post as senior partner of the firm."

A couple days later, a knock came at his door at home. Hemmingsen's wife, who was preparing for work, opened it to find the president of the law firm standing there holding Jørn's letter in two hands. Inside, the man sat down in the couple's small, light-filled living room, and Hemmingsen's wife served coffee. Hemmingsen sat across from him and fidgeted nervously as his former boss gingerly posed questions. Had the firm somehow mistreated him? Was it an equity issue? Something else?

"No," said Hemmingsen, "I've just decided to leave."

Pulling Hemmingsen's wife aside, the president offered to pay for psychological counseling. But Hemmingsen declined with a smile. He knew what he was doing. "I realized my life was slipping away quickly," he said. "And it just terrified me."

In the ensuing months, Hemmingsen and his wife sold their big house in the city and bought a smaller one on the edge of town. Hemmingsen traded in his Mercedes for a bicycle. He whiled away his afternoons reading books on history and art. He meditated. Six times a week he ran ten kilometers around a nearby lake. In the early evening, he'd share a glass or two of wine with his wife and talk about her day. He didn't have much to report.

One day, while perusing the newspapers, he noticed an ad for a warehouse position at Ikea. The job involved driving a forklift and lifting crates. He applied for the job. The warehouse manager looked at his résumé and, noticing his 18 years at a prestigious law firm, asked why he was applying for a warehouse job.

"Have you been in jail, or something?"

"No, I just want to work with my hands," Jørn replied, outstretching his arms in a gesture of explanation.

Hemmingsen got the job and began a new chapter in his life. He started at Ikea as a warehouse worker, hoisting boxes onto shelves and finding great satisfaction in the manual labor. He lost 15 pounds. Within a year, he was promoted to warehouse manager, another new challenge at which he excelled. But within 18 months of this promotion, he tired of managing people. So he quit again. And once more he found himself confronted by a boss bewildered by his decision to leave.

"I'm glad I did it," he said, recalling the experience. "But it wasn't my true passion."

So Hemmingsen opened up a small practice as a counselor, where he now works from 9 a.m. to 1 p.m. As a mediator, he helps families to stay together or to separate peacefully. It's work that addresses his values, he says, but also leaves him time to pursue his hobbies and health.

I met him at his office one afternoon to bike with him back to his house. He didn't actually invite me. I just asked if it would be okay, and after demurring, he said, of course, no problem. A thin, athletic man with a handsome, owlish face, he speaks with a quick wit that turns his fractured English into an almost poetic use of language. When I asked him why he changed jobs, for example, he replied, "Because I was looking for a new string on the instrument of my life."

Setting off through the city, we pedaled a few hundred yards over cobblestone streets, across a highway, and then, abruptly, into nature. Taking a bike path through a forest, we crossed several bridges and finally arrived on the shores of Brabrand Lake, about two miles outside of town. Halfway around the lake, Hemmingsen stopped his bike and pointed to a pathway into the forest. We dismounted and followed the path to a clearing and a small dock. "Here, I meditate every day," he said.

At his house, Hemmingsen poured me a soda pop called Squash and we sat out on the patio. There he explained why he and his wife are still in love after 30 years, even though they have totally different hobbies and values. When he takes

The Joy of Exercise

People living in thriving countries tend to participate in a physical activity 1 to 2 times each week, according to the Gallup World Poll. Those who participate in even small amounts of physical activity report smiling more, or being treated with respect on a regular basis.

hiking trips into the Austrian Alps, for example, his wife never joins him. "She's a shopper," he explained. I asked him if he was sorry she didn't go. "No," he shot back, cutting off my question. "She would never stop talking." While this doesn't sound like the type of response you'd hear from a happy man, he explained that he appreciated living with someone different. "Two of me wouldn't have worked," he said.

Since Hemmingsen has run 250 kilometers a month ever since he quit his full-time job, I thought I might learn something about him by joining him on a run. As we trotted down his driveway to the lake path, I noticed that he cantered more than ran—he had this bouncy but fluid gait, like running on springs. I'm a fit guy and have tried to retain some of the conditioning from my long-distance bicycling days, so I figured I could easily keep up with him. After all, he was almost 20 years older than I. But after galloping the first kilometer of our ten-kilometer sprint, I was hurting and bargained him down to five. He agreed readily.

"Do you always run this fast?" I asked, wheezing and panting. I had been bragging about the world records I held for cycling across the Americas and Asia. He looked at me and cocked his head questioningly.

"No," he said. "I usually run much faster."

I'm thinking, he's giving me a line of bullshit. So, I say, "Why don't we run at your pace then. I'll keep up."

"This is fine," he replied matter-of-factly. And with that, he kicked up his pace to a seemingly effortless dash. For me this felt like an all-out sprint. My thighs burned. My knee ached. I felt like I was going to exhale my lungs. I kept up with him for no more than 15 seconds, after which he disappeared around the curve of the lake, a hundred meters ahead. By the time I finished the lap, he had already showered and was drinking an orange juice on his deck.

He poured a glass for me.

"You kicked my ass," I said, still panting.

"Please," he replied. "That kind of talk will never make a Dane happy."

Lessons from Denmark

Some people say Danes are happy because they have low expectations. Not true. If they don't aspire, on the whole, to accumulate great wealth or to achieve world dominance, what they do expect in terms of education, health care, social interaction, and exposure to the arts far outstrips what Americans expect. The Danish path to happiness, after all, isn't about aspiring to scale peaks but rather about the satisfaction that comes from living at a high plateau. It's about thriving in an environment that nudges them away from superficial pleasures and toward lasting—and sometimes counterintuitive—activities that bring authentic happiness.

Build an Environment of Trust

Worldwide surveys show that the Danes are among the most trusting and trustworthy people on the globe. In Århus you can leave your baby carriage (and baby) parked outside a café and not have to worry. Of course, trust works two ways. Danes also strictly obey laws. A pedestrian in Copenhagen will wait patiently at a crosswalk until the light turns green at four in the morning even if there isn't a hint of traffic. Business works more efficiently and better when people can trust each other. That may explain why Denmark is also one of the richest nations per capita. The lesson: Live in trustworthy places, surround yourself with trustworthy friends, and be trustworthy yourself.

Tolerance

Tolerance of other races and lifestyles correlates with happiness in many national surveys. The Danes were among the first to give women the vote, to allow gays to marry, and to permit pornography. Some might label these policies as permissive, while others simply point to the history of civil rights in place like the United States, where as recently as 1950, it was a radical idea for a black person to marry a white person—or even to sit at the front of a bus.

Seek Status Equality

In Denmark, modesty is a virtue. Here the garbage-man fits seamlessly into an upper-class neighborhood, the businessman sits in the front seat of a cab. In some parts of the world, people feel the need to compete with their neighbors to possess a bigger house, a nicer car, or more fashionable clothes. Here there's no pressure to keep up with the Joneses; in fact, you lose points by showing off. The lesson: Look for neighborhoods where people are about as rich (or as poor) as you are. Build your social circle with those who accept you and don't make you feel that you need nicer clothes, a bigger car, or anything more than what you already have.

Seek Economic Equality

With one of the lowest disparities in the world between rich and poor, Denmark devotes about half its annual budget to smoothing out society's inequalities. That might be a lesson for other nations. Economic equality contributes to a sense of security. One caveat: Danes also possess a Protestant work ethic and are inclined to work hard independent of financial incentives.

Care for the Young and Old

Danes spend more money per capita than almost any

other nation on their children and the elderly. Young people get an excellent education and health care. Equipped with a strong liberal arts education, they make productive employees. Older people are similarly well cared for. Adults spend little time worrying about retirement and focus more on pursuing the jobs they love. Older people can enjoy their final years with the knowledge that the necessities will be covered. It's a virtuous circle.

Freedom

There's a complex relationship between happiness and freedom. Children here are taught from an early age to make up their own minds, kids call their teachers by their first names, and freedom in general is cherished. This freedom teaches people how to make good decisions. They are free to try out a job and fail, as a social safety net will catch them. They are also free to speak their minds, and for the most part to do what they want. This is all tempered, of course, by a sense of social responsibility and a solid work ethic.

Get the Right Job

Most of our waking hours are consumed by our jobs. In the United States, many people chose a job based on how much it pays or how much it will impress their friends. In Denmark, where taxes consume most of people's wages, and ambition is frowned upon, there's no upside to taking a job for pay or status. So people take jobs that interest them, which gives them a better chance to feel satisfaction and flow in their careers. Danes specialize in furniture design, niche technology, art, and architecture—creative, challenging careers that stimulate the kind of engaged happiness that psychologist Mihály Csíkszentmihályi calls "flow."

Work Just Enough

Most Danes work 37 hours a week and go home to their families or their associations. They take an average of six weeks of vacation. If people work for money, they do so to get just enough. The lesson: Knock off at 5 p.m. and take your vacations. The Danes' Protestant work ethic is tempered by their understanding that working too hard—or too long—is a waste of time. So they get their jobs done and pursue other things they enjoy.

Cultivate the Art of Living

Proactively develop an appreciation of art that will last a lifetime. Denmark's visionary educator and philosopher Nikolai Grundtvig launched folk schools that gave the sons and daughters of peasants a liberal arts education in literature, music appreciation, and art. They also learned the art of conversation. Today, there are still more than 90 state-subsidized folk schools where people of all walks of life can develop their love of the arts.

Make Cozy, Well-Lit Home Environments

Winters are long and dark in Denmark, where night falls by 4:45 on November afternoons. To compensate, Danes have created cozy environments with candles, the warmth of the hearth, and the gathering of friends.

Nudge People into Interaction

While Danes are not particularly outgoing, they have a tradition of joining associations and volunteering—19 of 20 people belong to clubs as varied as rabbit jumping, cold-water swimming, and handball. These clubs make a big difference in a nation where isolation means unhappiness.

Optimize Cities for Activity

It's hard to be happy when you're unhealthy. Danes tend to be fit, with lower body mass indexes and lower rates of obesity than some of their European neighbors. Danish cities are designed so it's easy to walk or bike from one place to another. With a 30-minute walk, you can travel from the cobblestone center of Copenhagen all the way to the queen's castle, which doubles as a park, or to the sea, where people swim and sail, or to the woods on the edge of town. Recreation is accessible to everyone. The lesson: Make walkable, bikeable cities with high-quality parks a priority, not an afterthought.

Volunteer

More than 30 percent of Danes volunteer their time to benefit their communities. This makes for a healthier society and helps people take the focus off their own troubles. Michael Artmann, the unemployed welder with a grade school education, still finds time to enhance his life through volunteering.

Use Taxes

No one loves Denmark's high marginal tax rate, but surveys show they tolerate it. As a result, everyone has health care, young people are nudged into education because it's free, and all citizens have a safety net should they find themselves down on their luck or eager to find a job that better suits them. High taxes on energy use have spurred investment in renewable energy. In 2006–2007, Denmark had the largest greenhouse gas emission reductions of EU countries, 6 percent. Renewable resources currently supply almost 30 percent of Denmark's electricity.

CHAPTER THREE

Singapore:
Can You Manufacture
a Happy Nation?

Joyful relatives surround a bride and groom at a Malay wedding in Singapore, where as many as 2,000 guests may be invited, emphasizing the importance of social networks in the Malay community. PHOTO BY DAVID MCLAIN/AURORA

Singapore:
Can You Manufacture
a Happy Nation?

*It does not matter what color the cat
as long as it catches the mouse.*
—Proverb

Many travelers to Singapore begin their visit at Changi
International Airport, a sprawling, sanitized compound
where bright lights, crisp guards, polished brass, and crys-
tal cut glass create a Disney-esque air of cleanliness and
efficiency. Glaring signs show you the way to customs and
immigration. They also warn that no photography, smoking, or gum chewing is allowed. After you wait in a very
short line, a customs guard dressed in a stiff blue uniform
with epaulets greets you with a regulation smile, offers you
a mint, and mechanically stamps your passport. Then a gag-
gle of politely predatory taxi drivers meets you in the terminal. They hawk rides to any destination on this island
nation for a $35 flat rate.

My driver turned out to be a fiftyish woman in cat glasses and black tights. Her taxi, a spotless fire-engine red Mercedes adorned with little stuffed animals, bobblehead trolls, and rhinestone windshield trim, was purring at the curbside. She popped the trunk, which neatly held everything one might need to either fix a flat tire or host a picnic, and loaded my bags. Then she scurried around to open the door for me. As we whisked down the tree-lined street through a forest of high-rises, I noticed that neatly manicured shrubs stood like soldiers along the highway. "We're very proud of how clean our country is," my driver offered in Chinese-accented English. "We've had much public education to remind us not to litter."

"Your government must spend a great deal of money to keep these shrubs and trees so trim," I commented. She just shrugged.

"It's public education."

She told me she was a widow and lived in an apartment with her mother, since her siblings were all married. "Of course, if I had more money, I'd like to live by myself, and then I could do as I pleased," she remarked. I asked if her mother cooked or cleaned, or if there were any other benefits to her living in her mother's house.

"No, it's our tradition to have parents live with children," she said. "It's our duty."

"But if you had the money, you'd live on your own?"

"No," she said finally, changing her mind.

When we arrived at the Sheraton, a white-gloved doorman offered to take my backpack, and the front desk staff greeted me with the same smiling efficiency that I'd encountered at customs. In my room I found a letter signed by the general manager, who expressed his desire to make my "lodging product" of the highest quality. I unpacked, showered, slipped on the hotel's complimentary, cellophane-wrapped cotton slippers, flicked on CNN, and settled in to enjoy my lodging product.

I was starting to see what people meant when they said that Singapore takes some getting used to.

Months earlier, when I'd first started thinking about visiting Asia's happiest place, I'd assumed I'd be booking a plane trip to Tibet, where I'd hang out with Buddhist monks and followers of the Dalai Lama. Or that I'd be winging my way to Fiji with its sun, sugar sand beaches, and sensual native charms. Or perhaps I'd hike to Bhutan, the tiny, mountainous country between India and China, whose king famously downplayed the concept of gross national product as a measure of national wealth in favor of an index of gross national happiness.

But one of my chief consultants, sociologist Ruut Veenhoven, had steered me away from the usual places. Too often,

Singapore Facts

Region: East Asia

Location: Island city-state located off the southern tip of the Malay Peninsula about 85 miles north of the Equator

Population: 5.1 million people

he said, the places we imagine as paradises don't measure up when it comes to basic prerequisites for happiness, such as decent food, basic shelter, adequate health care, and mobility. Such places suffer from what Veenhoven calls the "happy native" myth. Tourists who come for a few weeks to enjoy the stunning beauty or effusive hospitality of the local people see colorfully dressed kids laughing and playing and assume that they live in a stress-free paradise. What the tourists don't see is that the same kids have a parasite in their bellies and no hope of getting a decent education, that Dad is stuck in a job he hates, and that Mom is secretly abused.

No, Asia's true happiness hot spot is a 40-mile-long island nation on the southern tip of the Malay Peninsula, Veenhoven had said. He was talking about Singapore, of course, home of 5.1 million people and 250 or so shopping malls. With one of the highest population densities in the world—more than 19,000 people squeezed into every square mile—Singaporeans live vertically in skyscrapers and high-rises. Expectations about the quality of life have risen, too; workers put in long hours in pursuit of the five C's: cash, credit card, car, condominium, and club membership. Known as a society of workaholics, Singapore has also become famous for its paternalistic government, which strictly enforces laws on the most trivial of infractions, from chewing gum in public to failing to flush a toilet. Offenders convicted of crimes from selling heroin to spraying graffiti on a wall are strapped to a wooden frame so a caning official can deliver flesh-splitting lashes with a soaked rattan switch, leaving a bloody pool on the floor.

Singapore: Can You Manufacture a Happy Nation?

And this place is happy?

Yes, it is, Veenhoven had insisted, at least by Asian standards. Independent studies conducted between 2000 and 2009 reported higher levels of happiness in Singapore than in any other Asian nation. The World Values Survey found that 95 percent of people in Singapore said they were very happy or quite happy. In 2005-2009, the Gallup organization interviewed a cross section of people in each of more than 130 countries around the globe. Citizens were asked to rank their current circumstances on a scale of 0 to 10, with 10 being the "best possible life." Researchers asked Singaporeans if they were well rested, treated with respect, experienced smiling or laughing, engaged in learning or interest, or felt enjoyment, and also about "negative experiences," including physical pain, worrying, sadness, stress, depression, or anger, to arrive at a measure of daily experiences. Singaporeans rated a 6.9, and only 2 percent reported feeling depressed. Of all the people of Asia, Veenhoven had said, the citizens of Singapore were definitely the happiness rock stars.

Still, my first impression of Singapore was one of a well-scrubbed, shrink-wrapped nation of march-in-step people hell-bent on getting ahead. Could such people really be happy? Yes, the experts said. "People tend to be skilled at monitoring their own emotions and generally know how intensely they are experiencing happiness," write psychologists Ed Diener and Robert Biswas-Diener in *Happiness: Unlocking the Mysteries of Psychological Wealth*. "We refer to 'happiness' as 'subjective well-being' in scientific parlance, because it is about how people evaluate their lives and what is important to them. An individual's subjective well-being is often related to some degree to his or her objective circumstances, but it also depends on how people think and feel about these conditions. Subjective well-being encompasses people's life satisfaction and their evaluation of important domains of life such as work, health, and relationships." What makes one person happy might not be the same for someone else, in other words. People in different cultures value things differently. For the purposes of comparative analysis, therefore, a measurement of subjective well-being is the most reliable information we have about happiness.

As the polls confirmed, people in Singapore reported being happy. Was it possible that, for some reason, they weren't being honest in the surveys? Were they worried, for example, that their government might disapprove if they said they were unhappy? Perhaps. Studies have shown that individuals in Asian cultures can be sensitive about how they present themselves to other people. But if Singaporeans wanted to fib

Subjective Happiness

The term "subjective well-being" includes a combination of happiness, peace, fulfillment, and life satisfaction. In short, it is a snapshot of how a person perceives his or her own happiness.

about their happiness to the Gallup people, why stop at a 6.9 and not push the meter to a 7.5 or a 9? If there was some sort of subtly programmed compulsion to make the country look good, or to avoid acknowledging that people work too hard, a 6.9 out of 10 is not that convincing. And what about other Southeast Asian nations? Singapore's results are in line with the culturally similar countries of that part of the world. This suggests that either the respondents from the entire region are fibbing collectively—but in a not very dramatic way—or they are generally giving honest assessments of how they feel. Happiness researchers see consistencies of that sort as another reason to trust survey results.

But even if we were to accept that Singaporeans really are happy, the big question remains: Why? And what can they teach the rest of us?

EVEN ARTIFICIAL SNOW

The next day, I struck off into the wilds of downtown Singapore. Getting around was easy. Subways are punctual and immaculate, and walkways are clearly marked with pictures, signs, and maps on every block. Forget how to use the stairs? At both the top and the bottom of the stairway, explicit directions remind you to stay to the right and to take one step at a time. Three thousand buses stop at over 4,500 bus stops on the island. Need a taxi? Nearly 20,000 of them prowl the streets and are ready to take you anywhere. In case you're still at a loss, omnipresent eager-beaver police officers are quick to help.

Thrive

I wandered by some of Singapore's famous hawker stalls, the sterile food pavilions that the government created to get pushcarts and street vendors off the street. Imagine a huge, spotless picnic area surrounded by food stands serving fantastic exotic items: tiger prawns, "morning glory" greens with shrimp paste, chili-encrusted stingray, oyster omelets, duck in plum sauce, lemon-accented cane juice, mango pudding, and more. Each sparkling stand had garish pictures of food offerings with slightly misleading prices (the shrimp was advertised as five dollars per 100 grams, but the smallest shrimp weighed 200 grams). As soon as I walked in, vendors pounced on me, thrust a menu at me, and led me to a table, whether I followed them or not. This was my first exposure to Singapore's famously aggressive can't-lose attitude. The service was surly but efficient; the food was good.

Later I walked down to Orchard Road, the old colonial thoroughfare that serves as Singapore's Times Square-meets-Piccadilly Circus—a reminder of the country's British roots. At the beginning of the 19th century, this had been little more than a fishing village. In 1819, British statesman and amateur naturalist Sir Thomas Stamford Raffles negotiated a deal with local chiefs to secure the newly minted enclave on the southernmost tip of the Malay Peninsula for the British Empire. Within decades, it grew into one of the empire's most prosperous settlements, attracting immigrants from China, India, and Malaysia. By the 1940s, this merchant class was asserting its voice; the tiny nation was preparing to stand on its own.

Singapore: Can You Manufacture a Happy Nation?

Now, as I strolled down the country's main street, I experienced neither British stuffiness nor the crazy smells and noises one might expect of Southeast Asia. Instead, a unique hybrid culture had emerged. It was a December evening, and great crowds of orderly people—mostly of Chinese descent but also Malay, Indian, and a few white expatriates—moved down packed streets like a human tsunami. Shopping malls brandishing names like Ralph Lauren, Hermès, Mont Blanc, and Todd dominated the landscape. The Four Seasons Hotel advertised a $90 Sunday brunch. A line snaked out of the Gucci shop. For what, I wondered. A blue light special on loafers? Outside one mall, "snow" fell surrealistically on an enormous Christmas tree and a stunned crowd. Great snow guns shot granulated suds into the air, and they sifted down onto shrieking, gleeful children and their fawning parents. A nearby sign blinked the time and temperature: 6:43 p.m. and 36°C (97°F).

Was this what happiness meant in Singapore? Expensive gifts and artificial snow? After my first couple of days on the island, I was beginning to ask myself if anybody in so manufactured an environment could really be happy. It seemed to me they had all the trappings of success but none of the soul. If Singaporeans were telling researchers they were happy, maybe they were just deluding themselves.

FIRST PIECES OF THE PUZZLE
To test my hypothesis, I paid a visit to Dr. Tan Ern Ser's cluttered office at Singapore's Institute of Policy Studies. As his

nation's representative for the World Values Survey, Tan had collected more than 1,500 surveys to determine the nation's well-being and associated values. He had also spent a good bit of time in the United States at Cornell University and the University of Michigan. The day I met him, he was wearing a casual shirt, gray slacks, and comfortable loafers. We exchanged a few pleasantries and talked about his children and how he likes to take them to the zoo on the weekends. Then he showed me his own list of the values and priorities that he felt were most closely associated with well-being in Singapore. Good health, a feeling of public safety, and a regard for family topped the list. Environment and politics were at the bottom.

"Happiness here is largely rooted in the fact that the government has seen to the fundamentals of well-being," said Tan, speaking in careful sentences tempered by academic rigor and an understanding that in this nation, too much candor in certain matters can cost you your job. The country is "well run," he went on to say. Government ministers in Southeast Asia are often underpaid and on the take, he added. But in Singapore, they're often trained in American Ivy League schools and paid seven-figure salaries. Bribery carries harsh penalties (which may help explain why, according to Transparency International, Singapore has one of the world's lowest rates of corruption). There is almost no severe poverty, he said. Compared to other parts of Southeast Asia, there are also relatively few ethnic problems (in Tan's surveys, 90 percent of Singaporeans said they were proud to be Singaporean). The fact that English is the lingua franca also puts the major ethnic groups on an equal footing when it comes to communication. Housing laws also promote mixing of ethnic groups. In every public housing high-rise, 77 percent of the residents must be Chinese, 14 percent Malay, and 8 percent Indian, reflecting the same proportions as the general population. So there are no ethnic slums.

"But what about all of the petty rules?" I asked. "What about the laws fining people who spit, chew gum, or forget to flush the toilet? Doesn't the fact that the government can litigate you into the poorhouse for expressing political dissent bother people?"

"People do grumble about the rules," Tan said. "But the government goes out of its way to explain why they're in place. Over time, the annoyance eases, and pretty soon we just adapt. Now most people just take them as part of life, and we reap the benefit of not stepping on gum or someone else's phlegm. We have flush toilets that work. People like freedom, but they also like stability and security. All societies are trying to find that happy medium, and our country has done a pretty decent job at it. My theory of happiness is that if you're hopeful and confident of getting what you want in life, then you are happy. If you feel like your path is always blocked, then you're not going to be happy. Singapore makes sure your path is not blocked." From Tan's point of view, people in Singapore are willing to give up certain freedoms to gain greater safety and opportunity.

For another perspective, I traveled across town to meet Dr. Ho Kong Weng, an economist at Nanyang Technological University. Ho had just completed his own round of studies on happiness, which suggested that religious people are less concerned with money than nonreligious people, and that the most important predictor of whether a child will be happy is the happiness of his or her mother. When I asked Ho why Singapore outperforms the rest of Asia in terms of happiness, he pointed first to Singapore's remarkable economic growth. During the past 40 years, he said, the wealth of the average Singaporean has multiplied 11 times—the fastest growth of any economy in the history of the world. By offering generous tax breaks, Singapore has lured multinationals to invest in the small nation. Meanwhile, Singapore has made huge investments in domestic universities and grants to enable scholars to study abroad. The government also has made it easy for foreign immigrants to enter the country and fill new jobs. The ensuing upward spiral has created a feeling of constant progress toward the "good life," Ho said. For a society obsessed with achievement, Singapore's economy has supremely "unblocked the path to perceived happiness." On top of that, he said, Singapore has one of the world's lowest levels of unemployment, and the differences between rich and poor have remained relatively small. "Though we have a number of very rich," he said, "the overwhelming majority of Singaporeans are middle-class, and they set the standard, which is good. It's very clear from world data that inequality has a negative impact on happiness," he said.

That made sense to me. The promise of prosperity tends to make anyone happy. I'd also heard that Singapore owes at least part of its high happiness quotient to its strong family ties. To help keep families together, the government offers tax subsidies to citizens who care for aging parents. Partly as a result, 84 percent of seniors live with their children. That makes all family members feel like they're part of a legacy, rather than just lonely individuals.

I had one more name at the top of my interview wish list: the elusive master architect of Singapore's society, Lee Kuan Yew. As a young firebrand in 1959, the Cambridge-educated lawyer suddenly found himself in control of a new society. During his first six years in office, he steered the country through uneasy alliances with both communist China and Malaysia. When Singapore finally achieved independence on August 9, 1965, Prime Minister Lee broke down and cried at a press conference. But these weren't tears of joy. He had actually fought hard to keep Singapore connected to Malaysia because he believed that his nation was too small to

Asia's Happy Places

When residents of Asian countries were asked to reflect on current life satisfaction, these countries reported the highest levels according to Gallup: 1. Singapore, 2. Japan, 3. South Korea, 4. Thailand, 5. Indonesia, 6. Taiwan, 7. Malaysia, 8. Myanmar, 9. Vietnam, 10. Bangladesh.

survive in the gladiator ring of the free world. With no natural resources, no real industry, an ominous proximity to heroin-producing countries, and a prickly relationship with its much bigger—and closest—neighbor, Malaysia, Singapore seemed to have the deck stacked against it. Moreover, its population was made up of three disparate cultures—Chinese, Malay, and Indian—creating fertile ground for ethnic tension. Considering this backdrop, how could this neophyte country survive, let alone achieve Asia's highest levels of happiness? I was dying to ask the man who had led the way.

After several months of pursuing an interview through official channels, however, I'd gotten nowhere. Even after I arrived in Singapore, people told me it was impossible. Lee had complained about being burned too many times by Western reporters who lambasted him for the government's strict laws. "Expect several months for a reply," Lee's office had told me.

So I turned my attention to finding a few examples of Singapore's self-proclaimed happy citizenry.

A PERFECT LIFE (ALMOST)

One evening, at the suggestion of photographer David McLain, I caught up with Celina Lin at a posh restaurant near the water. McLain had shot her portrait a few days earlier and had come away impressed by her story. "You have to meet her," he had said. "She's a self-made millionaire, socialite, and a beauty—the perfect picture of Singaporean success."

It was still early when I arrived at il Lido restaurant. The crescent-shaped dining room fused contemporary

Singapore: Can You Manufacture a Happy Nation?

Danish furniture with faux Romanesque columns and floor-to-ceiling windows that displayed a 180-degree sweep of Singapore Strait. The urban pulse of techno music was just audible over the subdued din of the young moneyed class who were chasing down seared scallops with pomegranate martinis to fortify themselves for the night ahead. Lin was sitting at the bar. She wore a low-slung, lavishly embroidered gold top, tight-fitting designer jeans, and high heels. She had a delicate face with a small, expressive mouth and flawless alabaster skin, framed by shoulder-length black hair and diamond-flecked chandelier earrings. She was holding a flute of fine champagne languidly off to one side.

I knew a few things about Lin already, as I had read a profile of her in a local magazine. She'd been named as one of the ten individuals who "exemplify power in Singapore." After rising through her country's fiercely competitive academic ranks to earn a degree in psychology from the National University of Singapore, she'd turned to banking. For seven years, she'd worked as a broker and currency trader, often swimming upstream against the male-dominated current of Singaporean finance. At age 29, with one bold and brilliant currency bet, she'd secured a personal fortune. That had allowed her, as she told the magazine, to retire to "dedicate myself to the arts and self-development." She had bought a Porsche and a downtown condominium that she decorated with tasteful art and staffed with a live-in maid. Then, over the years, she had filled her closet with 300 pairs of shoes and clothes to match. Her attention to fashion and her friendships with designers had helped her win the title of one of "Singapore's 12 Icons of Style." A few months earlier, a film she'd helped make, *Singapore Dreaming,* was released to critical acclaim.

Now Lin was telling me about her current passion, a jewelry business. "I travel to fashion capitals every year, places like Milan, Paris, and Tokyo, and then interpret the trends into my work," she said in precise English, her second language. "We must have some food," she said, interrupting herself to beckon a waiter with a wave. "Pappardelle with duck ragout and black truffle," she ordered. "You should get Hokkaido scallops with asparagus," she said, and then ordered it for me. We talked for another 45 minutes. At precisely 8 p.m., she announced that she had to leave. The bill was mysteriously paid for.

"I'm going to a party. Would you like to join me?" she asked without waiting for a response. She knew the answer was yes.

We took a taxi to a charity ball at Sentosa Country Club, a Victorian nexus of luxury on a rare expanse of green. In a great hall, a Gatsby-esque jazz band was performing and Singapore's gowned and tuxedoed glitterati were dancing, cavorting, and exchanging gossip. Most of the party-goers appeared to be of Chinese descent, but there were also expatriates, mainly rising stars in the world of finance. Heads turned as Lin made her entrance, and she was immediately embraced by the hostess, a fiftyish doyenne in a long white dress and pearls. They chatted for a moment—mostly to exchange compliments—and then Lin launched into the party. Moving through the crowd like a goldfish among carp, she embraced friends and treated them to a flash of charm. Meanwhile, I happily assumed the role of an accoutrement, like a new handbag, as she introduced me around as her "friend from National Geographic." I soon realized that I was in charge of cleanup conversations, and I answered a few questions about my book as Lin moved on to the next acquaintance.

For a successful Singaporean like Lin, this was just another Friday night. On another day, the party might have meant hanging out with fashion designers at a sprawling nightclub that had once been a waterworks plant. Or the celebrity-filled opening of Singapore's first Gap store. Or a dinner party at the home of a Russian oligarch, where the tycoon's 12-year-old daughter dazzled guests with a Mozart recital. Having achieved the trappings of material success, Lin seemed to savor them richly. She was dedicated to her jewelry venture, to her friends, and to the fund-raisers she supported. What more could anyone want?

"Are you really as happy as you appear to be?" I asked.

"Of course," she shot back. But then, after a reflective pause, she demurred. "I am as long as I don't think of someone wealthier, having a more luxurious life, driving a bigger car, having a bigger house, having a wonderful husband who provides for her," she said. "When I think of that, I feel, I mean honestly, I feel a tinge of jealousy."

SPARRING OVER *PLAYBOY*

Jennie Chua was waiting for me in the chandeliered lobby of Singapore's famous Raffles Hotel, the 123-year-old hangout of legendary characters like Rudyard Kipling and Joseph Conrad. At the time, Chua was CEO of Raffles Holdings, Ltd., which owns and operates not only Raffles hotel but also 40 other hotels and resorts around the world. Routinely profiled in the Singaporean press as a model of success and philanthropy, Chua also held positions as chairwoman of the Singapore International Chamber of Commerce and chief corporate officer of CapitaLand, Ltd., the largest property developer in Southeast Asia, and sat on the boards of more than 20 other business, charitable, and educational organizations, such as her American alma mater, Cornell.

The first thing I noticed when we met were the marble-size pearls gracing Chua's neck, the glistening diamond clusters, and a gold ring cradling a dazzling sapphire—jewels that trumpeted, "I've succeeded!" As she sipped a cup of tea, she told me her story—the fishing-village roots, the hard-won education, divorce from a domineering partner, a knack for catering to Westerners' tastes, and a rapid ascent to CEO of Raffles Holdings—a story arc not unlike that of her tiny nation. As a respected civic leader at the top of her game, she'd gone well beyond the five C's of Singaporean success. Yet she still felt she had not arrived.

"Arrived is a difficult thing," she said.

When I asked her what made her most proud of her nation, she said it was that Singapore is clean and safe. A woman can walk through any neighborhood at midnight and not be afraid. Subways are immaculate and on time. Public toilets provide hand soap. And police officers are unfailingly quick to help.

Singapore: Can You Manufacture a Happy Nation?

"We've always focused on our children's future," Chua said when I asked her if Singaporeans were truly happy. "For so long, it was such a struggle to put a roof over our heads, food on the table, and get our kids educated. Today we have more things, but our values are the same. The five C's are just a more glamorous way to provide for our families."

A few days later, Chua invited me to the new condo she'd purchased one floor above her son's apartment. This time she looked grandmotherly, having eschewed her jewels for bifocals and a purple warm-up suit. She shuffled among answering my questions, unpacking boxes of expensive knickknacks, and keeping her two-year-old grandson from breaking them. I looked around at a lifetime of high-end clutter—an ivory chess set, intricately carved Chinese furniture, a teak jewelry box—and asked what she treasured most. She pointed to a simple, framed photo of her two sons, their wives, and her grandchildren.

"The generation of men who built this country barely knew their children," she said. "They had an enormous responsibility. They worked all the time and were fiercely competitive. The new generation has evolved and become less transactional. They spend weekends with their kids and are beginning to see the value of volunteering their time."

I wondered about this kinder, gentler Singapore. Poking a nerve, I reminded her of the lack of free press, the one-party monopoly, and the Friday canings. At this she stopped puttering and fixed me with the steely gaze of a woman who understood that all forms of happiness involve struggle.

"The idea that American democracy is the only path to freedom is arrogant," she said. "I'd rather live in a place where it's safe for my kids to play today than one where I can read *Playboy* tomorrow."

SINGAPORE'S HAPPIEST CORNER

It was one o'clock on a Saturday afternoon, and a wedding was about to take place in the open space beneath a 45-story apartment on the outskirts of the city. The midday sun was beating down with an equatorial ferocity that made the lawns, sidewalks, cement picnic tables, and neighboring buildings all look washed out, like an overexposed photograph. Enormous loudspeakers were blaring traditional music, like an overamplified snake charmer's horn run amok. The bride's father, wearing a tunic, a baby blue shirt, and a lavishly embroidered gold lamé sash, greeted the first of some 2,000 guests. Men and women were shaking his hand; young boys bowed their heads and kissed his hand in a gesture of respect. Upon seeing me, clearly a foreigner, he welcomed me effusively and motioned me toward one of the long banquet tables.

"Enjoy!" he commanded.

Between the cement pillars that supported the apartment building, there was a diaphanous blur of pastels: women wearing purple, lime, baby blue, and crimson shrouds. Looking cool in the intense heat, men wore loose-fitting, two-piece suits that looked like pajamas. Servants were ladling steaming plates of curried mutton from a bubbling 220-gallon copper vat. At the far end of the alcove, the bride and groom sat on thrones under a gauzy, flower-crowned canopy. One by one, guests approached the newlyweds and tossed handfuls of perfumed rice.

This, too, was Singapore. The wedding party and their guests were mostly dark-skinned Malays, the ethnic group that first inhabited the island. Now they share their tiny country with large populations of both Han Chinese and Indians, whose hardworking cultural traditions have helped them to prosper in Singapore's go-go economy. Too often, some say, Malays today see the best jobs go to people from the other ethnic groups. Too often, others belong to the nicest clubs and make the most money. By contrast, it seems that Malays are more likely to end up with jobs like taxi driver or street worker; they are more likely to be nurses than doctors. Malay women arguably have it worst. As Muslims, it seemed to me, their religion also makes them beholden to their fathers and husbands.

So I was quite surprised to discover that, according to the latest survey data from Singapore, the Malays—especially middle-aged Malay wives (that diaphanous blur of pastels)—are the happiest of Singapore's three ethnicities, which makes them the happiest subculture in all of Asia.

What's going on here?

The Malays, according to the World Values Survey, are slightly more family oriented than the other ethnic groups and more likely to rank religion as the most important source of satisfaction in their lives. Nearly all Malays in Singapore are Muslims. One imam I met told me that the Koran urges its followers to be happy with what God has provided. This seemed to contrast sharply with what I'd seen of the Chinese acquisitive can't-lose mentality. On the first festive day of Shawwal, Muslim Malays go from house to house to visit relatives. They catch up with old friends and distant relatives, patch up old disputes if any have developed during the year, and exchange small gifts. By contrast, Chinese Singaporeans celebrate the new year by burning effigies and praying for good luck and fortune. One group seems to focus on increasing social equity, while the other seems to emphasize increasing material equity. If this sounds overly critical of the Chinese in Singapore, we should also recognize that, as a group, they deserve a lot of credit for helping to build their nation's economy into one that provides everyone with the basics: adequate shelter, food, health care, ethnic harmony, and security—enabling all Singaporeans to pursue their cultural priorities with the knowledge that life's necessities are covered.

SECRET INGREDIENT—KAMPONG SPIRIT

When I met him, Ahmad Nizam Abbas was a 39-year-old attorney straddling two worlds. On the one hand, he was born to a large Malay family that follows the traditions of Malay culture and religion. On the other, he was educated in England and now works among largely Chinese businessmen who wear Prada suits, live in private condos, and work 70 hours a week. "Singapore has a big advantage over the rest of Southeast Asia," he told me when I visited his 18th-floor law office downtown. "Here, it's a given that if you work hard, you'll be rewarded. But for Malays there exists a perception that they're not as hardworking as other groups or that their goals aren't as lofty. The fact is, it's not that they don't want the better things, it's just that they're happy with what they've achieved. Achieving wealth is not an all-encompassing goal. If you go to a Chinese funeral, they have paper cars and a paper house at the wake. But at a Muslim funeral you're just wrapped in a white cloth. You don't bring it to the next life."

The Malays have something called the Kampong Spirit, he said. "In the past, we used to live in fishing villages called kampongs, where we pulled together to help each other during times of adversity or disaster or during times of celebration, like preparing for a wedding. This notion still survives. When a Malay moves into a new flat, within a few days, other Malays in the neighborhood will quickly get to know them—this dates back to our fishing village roots. If something happens to a Malay household, within a few hours the whole Malay community will be there to lend its support. It's not that Malays have more friends than Chinese, they just socialize more."

Compare wedding traditions, he continued. A typical Chinese wedding has 200 to 400 guests, including immediate

The More the Merrier

Singaporeans really do have fun in large groups. Currently, they hold hundreds of mass participation world records including the largest laughing session, the largest badminton rally, and the longest lantern parade.

family members and business associates, and takes place in a rented hall. He said, "You almost never see that with a Malay wedding because they need room for 2,000 guests, including not only family but distant relatives and their friends. I may have not seen someone for six years, and I'll get an invitation to go."

Abbas also noted the Koran's injunction to be happy with what God has provided—a notion that fits well on several levels with what we know about the fundamentals of human happiness. Gratitude also comes into play; research shows that people are happier if they are grateful for the positive things in their lives, rather than worrying about what might be missing. Such an attitude would encourage Malays not to compare their wealth to that of their neighbors—a surefire way of making themselves miserable.

That was certainly the case with Norridah Yusoh, the 43-year-old housewife we met in Chapter One. Every day she counted her blessings—her husband and three school-age children. As a middle-aged Malay wife, she fit the demographic profile of the happiest Singaporean. She was also the veil-wearing Muslim woman who knelt before her husband each night and guiltlessly begged his forgiveness. More than two years after I first met her, at the time of writing this book, I called her back on the phone. I reached her on a Saturday morning. In the background, I could hear the clinking of plates and the voices of teenage children. Her family was finishing breakfast. I wondered if she even remembered talking to me on a rainy evening in Singapore. "I remember you," she said. "You were the American journalist who was so surprised to hear that I actually wanted to wear my headscarf."

"And do you remember what you told me when I asked you how happy you were?" I asked.

"Yes I do," she replied snappily. "And I'm still a 9.5."

HAPPINESS ARCHITECT

Three days before I was scheduled to leave, I hit the mother lode of Singaporean happiness wisdom. Despite all the warnings I'd gotten about how impossible it would be, I managed to secure an interview with the famously media-wary Lee Kuan Yew—Singapore's founding father. For three weeks I'd been working the phones, lobbying influential Singaporeans, and hounding Lee's assistant. Then, one afternoon, I called Lee's assistant's assistant and asked for an opportunity to present my case in person. "After all," I said, "this is a story about happiness, and we just want to profile the man responsible for it." The assistant told the other assistant, who told Lee, who said yes.

Lee's residence was fit for a founding father. In this high-density nation where a 500-square-foot condo can run over a million dollars, he lives on a five-acre compound. Despite the fact that Lee is generally revered in Singapore, a small army of guards patrols the place. Entering vehicles are put through a rigorous search. We were stopped several hundred yards from his home and driven the rest of the way in a government car.

After 20 minutes in a waiting room, I was led into Lee's sanctuary. Expecting a stiff, formal interview with a cool disciplinarian, I was greeted instead by a warm smile from a man in casual slacks, loafers, and a Mister Rogers sweater. A muted light illuminated his airy, wood-paneled office. Simple plum-blossom drawings decorated the walls. On his spartan desk sat only an appointment book and a computer. Missing were the many awards he'd received—the Woodrow Wilson Award for Public Service, London's Freedom of the City award, and the Order of St. Michael and St. George. It was a space of contemplation more than reflection. Late into his ninth decade, Lee retains a razor wit, and we'd barely begun the interview before a soft chuckle broke the ice.

We were sitting at a long meeting table next to Lee's desk. His assistant poured us green tea. I began by describing the World Values Survey and the World Database of Happiness and how they both point to Singapore as the happiest place in Asia.

"But they never tell me yet," he replied wryly. "They always tell me we aren't doing enough."

Lee and his team have often been credited with building one of the fastest economies the world has ever seen. (President Barack Obama recently praised Lee as a legendary figure "who helped to trigger the Asian economic miracle.") Coincidentally, as we've seen, Lee's team also seems to have created the happiest population in Asia.

"Were you thinking about laying the groundwork for a happy society when you first started planning Singapore in 1965?" I asked Lee. "Or were you just trying to build a secure state?"

"It was simpler than that," Lee said. "I had to make it work or we'd all die. Never in the history of man had an island, which was the center of the British Empire in this part of the world, seen its masters leave and become independent. They'd allowed Malaysia to be independent in 1957, but they'd kept Singapore back. They wanted it as a military base for eastern Suez. By the time they allowed us to rejoin Malaysia in 1963, the political demographics had already settled in favor of the Malays, who were over 50 percent there. Therefore it was going to be a Malay Malaysia.

"By our entry into the federation, it became 40 percent Malays, 40 percent Chinese, and 20 percent Indians and others. In other words, a rainbow coalition for a government. They did not want that."

"But you had a different vision," I said.

"Yes, so they asked us to get out. So this little island with no resources had to survive. The greatest driving force was to find a way to make ourselves relevant to the world, and in that way we survived. We had to be of relevance to the world. That relevance was economics: Our efficiency, our ability to provide a base for secure production, commerce, services, exploration of business opportunities in the region, logistics, hubs, transportation of people and goods, in every possible way."

"Did it turn out the way you hoped?" I asked.

"It has turned out, in the end, better than I'd hoped," he replied. "I could not have foreseen the speed at which technology would globalize the world. With the computer, the satellite, it is possible to move machines, people, ideas, money at greater and greater speed with more and more convenience. That gave us opportunities. In other words, the world became our market and not just Malaysia."

"Somehow, Singapore was better able to leverage technology than elsewhere?" I asked.

"The Malays in Malaysia decided to abandon English and go back to Malay," Lee said. "We decided to keep English and also teach each group's mother tongue, Chinese, Mandarin, Malay, whatever. That gave us an enormous advantage. We were linked up to the world and the region. They are now trying to go back to English in Malaysia, but they've lost the teachers and they've lost a generation. It's very difficult."

The decision to go with English probably also prevented increased rivalry among the ethnic groups in Singapore, I offered.

"Absolutely," he said. "At the time of independence, the Chinese Chamber of Commerce came to see me, and they told me that we should have Chinese as the national language. But I felt if we did that, we'd never have any progress because we'll be quarreling all the time. Let's choose a neutral language and nobody has an advantage, I said. English wasn't the mother tongue of any of the racial groups. It was the language of government under the British and the language of commerce. I did not foresee it would also become the language of banking, and of the Internet, so that was a bonus."

I wondered where he found his ideas for putting Singapore together. "Did you use some previous model, or did you invent it or evolve it as you went?" I asked.

"No, I don't think I could have invented it," he said. "I studied London first, how it went from the center of empire to the center of international commerce, without empire, how they transformed themselves. Then I studied Hong Kong, which is similar to us, an island. They were under British rule, protection, and connections, so they could do all kinds of things because the Bank of England covered them. We had to create all these platforms ourselves. But that gave us an indication of where we could travel. I studied other places like Malta and decided that wasn't the way to go. They were living off British aid and the tourists. That wasn't going to give us a future. So it was improvising all the time, learning from other countries, and adapting these ideas in an eclectic way to make it work in Singapore. It was trial and error."

"When you drive through Singapore at night, the city makes even New York look like a village," I said. "I'm wondering what you think about when you look at the skyline of Singapore and what it used to look like when you were a young man, and what is it today. How does that make you feel?"

"It is a reflection of how the world has progressed," he said. "If the world had not progressed in the way it did, we would never be what we are today. Because America, Europe, Japan progressed, we were connected with them, their businesses were based here. Aircraft flew in and out every day. You can go to any restaurant and ask for beef from Texas, France, if you like, Australia, whatever. We have become a center for all kinds of people and businesses. When you see the skyline today, it's not indigenous, if you cut off Singapore from the world, it will go back to the fishing village it once was. If you want an argument for globalization, as I told the first WTO [World Trade Organization] director, Singapore is the result of globalization."

"BASIC CULTURE" POLICIES

As I listened to Lee tell his story, it struck me that another factor that makes Singapore work is that key traditions have survived here. But I wondered how long they would last. "Singapore has managed to adhere to its Asian values, despite its Western ways," I said. "Do you think they'll disappear in the younger generation?"

"It's a risk," Lee said, "because once we educate them in English, they become more westernized because they're reading English, American, British, Australian, and Canadian, watching TV and films, and traveling the world. I think the westernization of our people is an inevitable trend. I'm hoping the family and the basic education will retain some core values.

"We teach two languages. It's a very heavy burden on the children, from kindergarten upwards. If you're Chinese, you learn English and Mandarin. If you're Malay, you'll learn English and Malay. It gives them a sense of place, where they come from, of course, with the Malays, religion, Islam. That gives them a certain anchor. With the Chinese, it comes with mother's milk that you must work hard. You must be thrifty. You must have a good education, and then you'll be able to live a good life. Then you must look after your parents just like your parents looked after you.

"This is what I would call basic culture, not high culture, but basic culture, what you do, what you're going to do, what is important, what is not important in life, right and wrong. Of course, with personalization some of it gets overlaid by westernization. For instance, the idea of putting your parents into an old folks home, which was unthinkable before, has now become a necessity because you have husband and wife who both work, earning good livings. So who's to look after the grandparents?

"We are having this shift. I think it's not just happening in Singapore. It's happening in China, too. They're also having two-income families."

"Does that worry you?" I asked.

"It worries me in the sense that we've got to find a transition into a new equilibrium which is not too cruel to the old. They go into the old folks home, they're isolated, and they're lonely. They have no family support. Yes, a nurse or care worker will come and change your clothes and feed you, but it's an empty life. So it's a problem. But there are two ways in which this is taking place—one, sheer lifestyle. For instance, now women do not want to get married too early. Why should they? They're educated. They're marrying later and later and

Family Matters

Family is at the center of social structure in Singapore. In this collectivist society, the term "family" includes not only those genetically related to each other but also friends and neighbors. This extended support system allows Singaporeans to thrive and care for one another in unique, encouraging ways.

having fewer children when they marry. Why? They want to see the world; they're in a comfortable life. That's a lifestyle change, partly economic, but partly seeing how other people live. They travel the world; they're educated in America, Britain, and Europe. They say, 'No, I want this kind of a life.' As a result we have a declining population. Luckily for us, there are a lot of Chinese from China and Indians from India who find Singapore attractive to come and study, stay, and work."

"So what do you think are the ingredients to Singaporean happiness?" I asked.

"What we set out to do was create a society which was efficient, orderly, well educated, cultivated, courteous, learning the arts, culture dance, music, et cetera, not just making a living and caring for each other," he said. "So we go out of our way to make sure we don't have an upper class. You won't see beggars in Singapore. You won't see ghettos in Singapore. It's by conscious effort. We know there is a lower five to ten percent of the population that cannot keep pace with modern life, at the speed with which we are progressing. So we have to carry them and make sure that they have a home. In fact, we more or less give them a flat so that they're not out in the streets. We find them some work. We make sure they have jobs. If the job doesn't pay enough, then we subsidize the utility bills, the conservancy charges, all the services that must be rendered. The alternative is to have them out on the streets.

"At the same time, we are very hardheaded in that we don't subsidize consumption. We subsidize education, housing, and then we give you assets. If you want to spend them on transportation, on sweets, candy, whatever it is, here is your charge, you sell it, you spend it, and you're poorer off. But we find that if we give them assets, they keep it because they want to have them for their old age and also to bequeath to their children. We refuse to give subsidies for consumption. We give subsidies where it is essential to give them a competitive edge— education, health, housing. Those are basics that enable a family to grow up healthy, educated, and able to hold jobs."

"I think sometimes the key to happiness isn't necessarily the easiest route," I said. "I would love to have one more question: Are you happy?"

"Happiness to me is a state of mind. If I'm happy and relaxed and don't fret about the future, then I think the future is going to become very cloudy. You have to be fairly comfortable with the present. Fretting about unexpected things that can happen or trends, which are going to overcome you and you've got to meet them. For instance, way back in the late eighties we already saw China was going to be a problem, sucking away investments from the region and from us. So we then quietly moved into areas where we thought they would not be able to compete with us for a long time, which is intellectual property, pharmaceuticals, life sciences. You don't want to go someplace and have your latest discoveries come out as genetic engineering. We have moved into those areas. For them to change the system, the rule of law, reclamation of property rights, law of contracts, that's going to take them one or two generations. Theirs is the rule of whoever is the government or magistrate, or the officer in charge. We moved into those areas where we believed it would take some time to be able to compete on the same platform. Even once everything was functioning, we could see that we were going to run into difficulties."

"So when you think to yourself, 'I want to have a relaxing afternoon,' what do you enjoy?" I asked.

"I enjoy a stroll in the park, in the gardens, and a swim before dinner," he said.

"Simple things," I remarked.

"You have to be engaged with the world," Lee said. "Yes, I know Singapore, but it's changing. Yes, I know America, but every time I go there it's changed, new people, new leaders, and new enterprises. Life means impermanence. That's a British axiom: There's nothing permanent in life. No living thing is permanent. If it's permanent, that means it has no life. That's the challenge of life. Are you able to keep on adapting to your changed environment?"

"Why is that so hard for people?"

"Because you become complacent, and you resent leaving your comfort zone," he said.

"Don't you think that's the default position of most people?" I asked.

"Yes, it is. But you've got to overcome that," he said. "That's the problem with governing a country. You've got to change policy, and suddenly you've got to tell large chunks of the population. At the present moment, about 20 to 30 percent of our population did not get an education that enables them to do the kind of jobs that we now get. They never finished high school. That's a problem. We tell them, 'You've got to go learn another skill.' So from sitting on the factory floor doing assembly jobs, all right, you'll ride this thing and clean up the floor. So we create jobs for them. It's a challenge, but what's the alternative? They do nothing, and we just pay them a living allowance? You'll both go down the drain. If you work, you might not get as much as you did before, but we'll make up the difference. We call it workfare, not welfare. We have seen what happens to countries that go for welfare. It becomes a black hole. Even Sweden now has decided to pay 51 percent of their income in taxes to spread across the population. So we say I'll give you this, but you work. You earn your keep, and I will 'top up.' It's a problem. They would prefer that the companies don't move to China, Vietnam, or India. But how can it be, because we've got to move on to higher-skilled jobs, which they cannot do, but their younger brothers, cousins, or children can do. We've got to look after them."

"I have the feeling that the younger generation doesn't have the appreciation or the discipline that the earlier generations had to build a nation," I said. "They seem to demand more freedom."

"The problem, which is not unique to us, it's happening with the Japanese," Lee replied. "Their younger generation is not as dedicated as salarymen as their parents were. But I think when push comes to shove, they will exert themselves because there's something in the depths of their subconscious that says, 'You can't take this lying down.' So I believe that when push comes to shove, the majority will say, 'We can do it. Our fathers did it. Our brothers did it. Let's do it.' But when everything is going fine, they say no. It's a problem. Every festival day I see $100,000 to $200,000 worth of fireworks. I would never do that. I'd build a club. I'd build a little dispensary or clinic. But for 20 minutes you see this spectacle in the sky or on your TV, and then we'll give you computer graphics. That's the only way to attract the crowds at the marina. The younger generation says, 'We can afford it. Let's burn it up.' It still hurts me."

ENGINEERING HAPPINESS

As we started to wrap up the interview, I told Lee about a few expeditions I'd led years ago to look into the collapse of civilizations such as the Maya and the Anasazi. Some experts have speculated that, right before the collapse, there was a period of prosperity when people forgot the hard work and the discipline that had gotten them where they were. "Do you think that might happen in Singapore?" I asked him.

"It's difficult here," he replied. "They know that this is a very small island on which an enormous superstructure is erected. If we don't tend to it regularly, this whole thing comes to a halt. You can't go back to your paddy fields. There aren't any paddy fields. This island started off with 120 fishermen in 1819. Now there are 5.1 million."

"Do you feel pride when you think about that, that you were the man, with the little spark in your brain, and a lot of hard work?"

"I wouldn't say that. I may have presided over it. I may have pushed certain major thrusts, but there was a whole team that did many things to put flesh on the bones, and then the people worked hard to get us there," Lee said. "If they did not learn, if they did not stretch from their native languages into English, learn to be engineers, architects, accountants, whatever, we wouldn't have made it. Yes, we created the schools, the polytechnics, the universities; we sent our best students abroad to the best universities in the world. But it was their effort."

"If you would ask Singaporeans, 'Why do you think this place is happy?' they'll almost always say security," I said. "This is a secure place. I'm wondering how important you think strict laws are."

"It's not just strict laws," he said. "Strict law enforcement and certainty of discovery and punishment. There are other Asian countries where you can be kidnapped, ransomed, shot, killed, and carnapped, everything. And yet our people go there because it's cheap? Why is it cheap? It's a different environment. And it's lawless."

"But you're clear in your mind that strict laws and enforcement deter crime," I said.

"Absolutely. Look, to have that you must have an incorrupt administration. Once you have a corrupt administration, police force, officers, it goes down the drain."

"So you're saying once it's broke, you can't fix it."

"No, I'm not saying that. Once it's broke it is very hard to fix it, but it can be fixed if you're determined and you push it right down. You have to start at the top and go down. You can't catch the people at the bottom and expect it to end as long as it's going on at the center or the top."

"You had the advantage of building a nation from the bottom up," I said.

"We had the advantage first of an immigrant population," he clarified. "They have left their secure moorings—China, India, Indonesia—and they have come here to make good. So they are more willing to change than people in their own countries. Immigrants and first- and second-generation descendants of immigrants are willing to try new forms to succeed. The Chinese have not succeeded in getting them to stop spitting. It's an ancient Chinese tradition. Hong Kong hasn't stopped it, but we have."

"Because the population is more malleable."

"Because the population is an immigrant population. You've come here to make good. You've left your family, your homeland. To make good you've got to have a secure place where people will find it attractive to come and do business and base their operations here. You've got to provide that kind of atmosphere, ambiance, and these conditions. If you start spitting and acting in a Third World way, then you are a Third World country."

By now, we had finished our tea. I looked around at Lee's airy office again and was struck by its complete absence of clutter. How suitably his own approach to work captured the very notion he was describing—living out the values he found important. In the course of an afternoon's conversation, he did not mention the pleasures of raising a family, or pride in the fact that his son had succeeded him as prime minister. That might be viewed as a common conceit of the ultrasuccessful, except that my interviews with other Singaporeans progressed along similar lines. It is a culture, for better or worse, where personal and professional identities tend to merge, where careers or businesses become all-consuming. I rounded off the interview by asking Lee about himself. Did the environment of well-being he created for Singapore work for him? I asked him to rate his happiness on a scale of 1 to 10.

"Personally," he said after a moment's reflection, "when I was prime minister I would say 5. Now I would say 6 because I don't have that day-to-day fret."

"And what would it take to get to 9?"

"Nothing would take me to 9," he said. "Then I would be complacent, flabby, and walk into the sunset."

THE DIFFERENCE BETWEEN EAST AND WEST

I came away from my interview with Lee with a better understanding of how, when it comes to perceiving happiness, some important factors appear to be cultural. To oversimplify things somewhat, Westerners seem to value freedom and individualism, while Asians seem to value respect for elders, a striving for harmony, and a zeal for hard work and making the family proud—a legacy perhaps of Confucius, the fifth-century B.C. Chinese philosopher. Such values are not unimportant in the West. They just don't seem to be etched as deeply as they are in what you might call the collectivist psyches of

Asians. For Asians, striving for personal happiness appears to be a vaguely impolite and selfish concept that falls somewhere near the bottom of a list of lifetime goals.

For Asians, the individual exists only in the context of his family and community. The individual is not separate. He is often driven toward perfection, but not for personal gain as much as to live up to societal expectations, and to make his mother proud. For Westerners, on the other hand, happiness is about personal achievement, freedom, and independence, rather than fitting in and marching in step. For Asians, happiness is defined by society rather than by individual expectations. If you fail to live up to what everyone else perceives as happiness, you are therefore unhappy. Furthermore, personal happiness can only get in the way of social relationships. By flaunting your bliss, you could create jealousy and social disharmony. That's why, for many Asians, personal happiness is "incomplete" happiness, because it comes at the expense

Millionaires Club

In 2008, Singapore had the highest concentration of millionaires in the world, with 8.5 percent of the country's households owning more than $1 million, according to the Boston Consulting Group. Additionally, as a group, Singaporeans total their assets at well over three and a half times the gross domestic product.

of social harmony, which means it just isn't worth it. Life is just better when there is a clear, socially determined path to follow, and you follow it. If Americans are encouraged to "follow their bliss," then Asians are wary about the possible downside of finding it.

Lee understood this. He and his clutch of advisers had created a society that enabled Singaporeans—and, to a certain extent, Asians—to excel. Given the nature of their cultures, he sensed that Singaporeans would accept a broad range of restrictions in return for physical and economic security, along with the promise of collective success. And he was right.

Just as good courts and regulatory systems were needed to encourage capital investment in Singapore, Lee had told me, strict laws were needed to keep the streets clean and to break the population of what he called the "ancient habit" of spitting. Some of the restrictions that seemed obsessive, like the rules against gum chewing, were necessary, he argued. And though foreigners might feel queasy about that way of doing business, Lee reasoned that they would almost certainly not bring their capital or businesses to an island that was unsafe, unpredictable, or unsanitary. So he and his team went out of their way to educate Singaporeans so that everyone not only knew the rules, but also knew the reasons for those rules. They cleared all the obstacles for people to seek a good education, to get a good job, and to master their task. Then he put policies in place to provide for elders.

Perhaps the time has now come, I thought, for a new generation of Singaporeans who can not only maintain the best of the core values from the past but also adapt to Western influence without getting sucked into a vortex of materialism. I thought of people like Ahmad Nizam Abbas, who worked all the time but still managed to attend every Malay wedding, or Jennie Chua, who personified the pursuit of the almighty five C's but now spends much of her time volunteering. Of the people I met in Singapore, though, the one who impressed me the most as an example of Singapore's potential future was a happy sushi king.

A NEW BRAND OF HAPPINESS

His name was Douglas Foo. I met him for breakfast one morning at the Sheraton Hotel. He had an eager-to-please smile and a round face with thick lips. In my notebook I wrote, "emanates joy like the full moon radiates light." He wore permanent-press slacks, simple black shoes, and a bottom-of-the line Rolex that peeked out the cuff of his pinstripe shirt. "I'm the product of a strict upbringing," he said when I asked about his personal history. "Once, I got sick at school and called my father to ask for a ride. Instead of coming to get me, he chided me for wasting ten cents on the call and told me to walk home. That's how I learned the value of money." Later, after high school, he tutored for 18 hours a day, in two-hour sessions, on his days off. He amassed $50,000, which he invested in a clothing factory, but soon he discovered that the Chinese could do it for cheaper.

Realizing that he'd be better off building a brand that he could own and control, he founded Sakae Sushi "to create a unique, high-quality, and inexpensive sushi dining experience for his wife," as his promotional materials assert. When he opened his first sushi restaurant in 1998, he printed out the menu on his computer at 4 a.m. the day of the opening. He was sushi chef, waiter, dishwasher, and cashier. His gimmick was a two-way conveyor belt that eliminated the need for servers. The restaurant was high-tech, with interactive screens at tables and slick decoration. People liked the fact that they could choose the sushi they wanted when they wanted it. No waiting to be served. He opened his second shop four months later, and his business rocketed from there.

The chain grew quickly to more than 100 restaurants. Today, Foo has more than 1,000 employees in Singapore alone. I sat in on a meeting one afternoon when he and his team were going over procedures for employees opening restaurants abroad. The meeting had the chatty ambiance of a *Sex and the City* luncheon with Big Brother Boss overseeing things. At one point, the head of Chinese operations, a serious, erudite woman of perhaps 30, asked for suggestions about a new sushi product that would appeal to the Chinese palate.

"How about chop suey sushi?" quipped one manager.

Led by Foo, the entire room burst out laughing. He had a big, openmouthed laugh that he delivered boldly with his head cocked back. Then, if someone looked at him, he'd laugh even harder. You could see his molars. Instead of acting like the all-knowing, must-win corporate chairmen of Lee's generation, Foo solicited input from his employees, who used words such as "compassionate" to describe him. He established a clever business model, peopled it with young, energetic employees who found purpose in the intersection of raw fish and emergent technology, and got behind those people to help them succeed. Rather then acting as a leader who marched out in front, he led from behind in the role of an enlightened servant.

After work, Foo typically attended fund-raisers or club meetings. In addition to being a Rotarian, he served on the board of several charitable organizations, including one that met the needs of seniors in his community. On the rare night when he had no commitment, Foo went home. Unlike the business titans of an earlier generation, who were more likely to spend their free nights unwinding in the brothel-like kara-oke bars, with their giggling, eager-to-please waitresses, he'd go home and wrestle with his children. Or stay up late talk-ing to his wife about the family or seeking her advice in busi-ness. The next morning he'd try to wrestle with his kids again before school.

When I had first called Foo, he'd told me that, despite all his successes, he was only just an 8.5 out of 10 on the hap-piness scale. "I'm still on the first rung of the ladder to suc-cess," he'd said. "My perspective on life is that 20,000 days are not much. I intend to do as much as possible during that time. But early in my career, I was so consumed with work, I seldom saw my son. I was worried that one day when I got home from a trip, he would call me 'uncle.' I didn't want that to happen. So I was there when my son swam his first stroke. I was there for his first day of school and when he graduated from kindergarten. I know how important kids are, and nothing will keep me from attending to them, not even business."

At the end of the day I spent with Foo, he invited me to dinner. It was 10 p.m., and he took me to a high-end place I call the High Altar of Sushi. He'd invited his wife, a stunning beauty, and one of his assistants. In a long, narrow private dining room, we sat at a teak table illuminated by candles. We started with a sushi mound atop shaved ice, or sea urchin, scallops, and toro tuna. Then we moved on to a soup with a white Japanese tuber and seaweed, and then on to the main course of Alaska king crab tempura, prawns, another plate of seared Kobe beef, and seared foie gras. We finished with a montage of desserts, including tofu cheesecake and spiced sherbet. It was a feast, with a shot of top-shelf sake accompanying each course.

"You work like a dog but live like a king," I said to Foo at the end of the meal.

"I never worked a day in my life," he corrected me. And then, sensing the irony of his reply, he tilted his head back, pinched his eyes closed, and unleashed one of his volcanic laughs. I didn't exactly see the humor in it, but to sit across the table from this young, high-powered executive positively quaking with glee, I couldn't help but laugh myself. When he settled down and opened his eye to see me laughing, it sent him right back into another paroxysm of joy. At that point, I noticed a warm trickle running down my face as I literally, involuntarily, cried tears of happiness.

Lessons from Singapore

Douglas Foo, in many ways, epitomizes a new kind of happiness in Singapore, one propelled by tradition but tempered by modern forces. So what can Singapore—a place engineered to be a utopia of sorts—teach the rest of us about happiness? Perhaps when it comes to policy, maximizing freedom does not maximize collective happiness. In Singapore, at least, a system has emerged that provides an almost comforting degree of certainty to its citizens: Here are the rules. Follow them. Work hard and you will succeed. Pursuing the good life may indeed provide some real, if fleeting, level of happiness. And it requires a certain economic baseline for us to really enjoy the things that matter: family, relationships, and spiritual groundedness. No wonder, here, that happiness and success have become so tightly intertwined.

Security Is Essential

In Singapore you'll find security cameras glaring at you constantly, and car alarms shriek if you exceed the speed limit. The canings and hangings seem draconian, but Singapore's politicians are adamant that such strict rules have been key to the country's economic success. Of the more than two dozen people I interviewed, all cited security as the most important factor in Singaporean happiness. Daniel Nettle, author of *Happiness: The Science Behind Your Smile,* theorizes that we are predisposed by evolution to favor safety over freedom. "The caveman who worries about where he'll get his next meal, finding a mate, and about the potentially dangerous tribe that lives over the hill is far more likely to get his genes into the next generation than the caveman who runs free and sits by the campfire," he writes. In modern-day Singapore, security has translated into a general acceptance of strict criminal laws and restrictions not just on the media, civil rights, and some religious practices—Christian Scientists and Jehovah's Witnesses are regarded as cults—but also on political opposition. But how do you justify the barbaric practice of caning, or of hanging a man if he's caught with a half ounce of heroin? A recent happiness study conducted in Afghanistan found that people living in areas with a moderate Taliban influence were actually happier than those outside the Taliban's control. After decades of war and turmoil, ordinary people craved security so much, they seemed to be willing to put up with the Taliban's heavy hand. Which suggests, as the Singaporean example clearly demonstrates, that, under certain circumstances, security can be more important to human happiness than even freedom. Or conversely, as the Buddhists say, maximum happiness does not mean maximum freedom.

Policies of "Basic Culture"

Lee Kuan Yew built his country on the ideals of basic culture over high culture. He set out to create a society that was efficient, orderly, well educated, and courteous with an appreciation for the arts and for citizens who cared for one another. Then he went out of his way to minimize an upper class. His policies favored thrift, education, health care, support for seniors, and development over consumption and blind growth. So every citizen's basic needs would be covered. In general, tax policies encouraged investment. Educational policies encouraged self-improvement. Social policies encouraged work. Unemployment, a sure cause of unhappiness, was largely nonexistent. Other policies that favored well-being:

- subsidizing home ownership to foster financial security and community stability

- making quality primary, secondary, and university education accessible and affordable to everyone

- taxing consumption of luxury goods like Swiss chocolate and Japanese gadgets

- addressing poverty with "workfare" instead of welfare. In accepting that some proportion of the population is going to need help, be willing to create jobs to give the otherwise idle poor something to do.

- "topping up" minimum wages with government subsidies so that all workers make a living wage

- offering top pay for high-ranking government officials to attract highly educated talent and to discourage corruption

- providing tax incentives to keep seniors living in their children's homes or neighborhoods

Strive for Status Equality

Singapore, despite its great wealth, is largely a middle-class society. Over 84 percent of the population lives in privately owned, government-built housing. Lee astutely made English the country's lingua franca. He made sure all races had equal access to education and jobs. The result was de facto homogeneity that helped Singapore's society run more smoothly and happily. While ethnic and religious differences have become lightning rods for dissent and violence in neighboring Philippines and Indonesia, ethnic harmony has been praised as one of the best parts of living in Singapore.

Build an Environment of Trust

Creating an environment of trust should be one of government's top goals. In Denmark, we saw trust flowing from a population of white Lutherans bonded by a common history and common values. Lee Kuan Yew's government manufactured trust among disparate immigrants with different cultural traditions by establishing a common language and strict laws. And he created that environment from the top down. Ministers were paid in excess of a million dollars a year to reduce the temptation of corruption. Singapore has also invested heavily in making people understand the rules, the consequences of breaking them, and the certainty of enforcement. On the flip side, Singaporeans trust the police, the courts, and, by and large, the government. As a result, it's easier for the country to attract foreign businesses and to keep them there.

Live Your Values

Perhaps the most provocative person I met in Singapore was a comedian named Kumar, a transvestite known for his barbs about local frustrations and lifestyles. "We're like puppets," he said of his countrymen. "We're groomed to follow the rules, and now we just do it blindly." Although he appears on stage in a dress, Kumar was wearing a canary yellow tank top, tight white slacks, and dark shades the day I interviewed him at his apartment. At first, the authorities tried to prohibit his comedy show, he said. But eventually they decided to just ignore him, despite his sly use of Singlish—a creole dialect combining Chinese, Malay, and English—to poke fun at the shallowness of island life.

"All we do in Singapore is eat, shop, and do hair," he said.

Though Singapore may still be far from a wide-open democracy, the younger generation may be less interested in the 70-hour workweeks and strict codes of behavior that their parents and grandparents lived by. Perhaps as they move into positions of authority, the government will tolerate more freedom of expression about its values.

However you sum up Singapore, values count. When I asked Dr. Ronald Inglehart, director of the World Values Survey, what the most important determinant of happiness was, he told me unequivocally, "The ability to live out your values." For more than 40 years, Lee's government has created an environment where people can live out their values about providing for their families and living up to society's expectations. Singapore has offered a system that neatly—often rigidly—defines an individual's place in society. It also provides the ethnic stability, personal security, and economic freedom for people to find the place that best suits their values. For the Chinese in Singapore, Lee told me, "hard work comes with mother's milk." The lessons learned are clear: Set your priorities and your values, and try to live your life through that lens.

That said, values are shifting in Singapore. The happiest people in Singapore today seem to be those who have chiseled time out of their overbooked days for their children and spouses. They volunteer to help others and seem to get more from the experience than just a status bump.

So what can Singapore teach the rest of us about happiness? Perhaps when it comes to policy, maximizing freedom does not maximize collective happiness. Unless we feel safe and secure, we'll never be able to pursue the other aspects of living that give rise to genuine happiness: family, relationships, and spiritual groundedness.

Then again, as Kumar says, maybe all we really need is a good hairdo.

CHAPTER FOUR

Mexico:
The Secret Sauce of Happiness

Felipe Gutierrez Gutierrez shares a laugh with family gathered around their kitchen table in the mountain village of Potrero, Mexico, where a unique brand of humor lightens a sometimes heavy load of daily challenges. PHOTO BY DAVID McLAIN/AURORA

Mexico:
The Secret Sauce of Happiness

The Chihuahuan Desert reaches across northeastern Mexico like a giant amoeba, gobbling up 140,000 square miles of the states of Chihuahua, Durango, Coahuila, and Nuevo León. If you were to stand at the edge of Laredo, Texas, and look south all the way to where the blue dome of the sky meets the shimmering, rusty brown horizon, this is what you would see: a rocky expanse dotted with cactus, creosote, peyote, and mesquite, cut by jagged basins and etched with trace roads used by cattle herders and *narcotraficantes*. It's the sort of terrain that stings your eyes like a sandy wind. Every year, tens of thousands of would-be immigrants make their way across this desert in search of a better life to the north. Many perish under the unforgiving sun. Farther south, the desert extends another 200 miles to the Sierra Madre Oriental and Mexico's giant industrial capital, Monterrey, a region known for breweries and cement factories. It's not the kind of place that suggests comfort, prosperity, or superlatives. Which makes it all the more surprising that, according to the best scientific data, this part of Mexico is the one of the happiest pieces of real estate in the entire Western Hemisphere. In fact, when asked by researchers, 59 percent of the people here rate themselves as "very happy."

"That's about 24 percent more than in the U.S.," said Ronald Inglehart, a political scientist at the University of Michigan and director of the World Values Survey.

Where does all that happiness come from?

To begin my search for answers, I flew to Mexico City to talk with the nation's leading experts. I was met at the airport by Jesús Lopez, a local photographer known as a master at handling logistics. He had agreed to moonlight on my behalf by setting up interviews and helping me get around. As he greeted me in the terminal, he offered a warm handshake and a mischievous smile. A short, middle-aged man with shiny black hair, platform shoes, and an untucked, body-hugging dress shirt, he looked like a cross between George Lopez and Dennis the Menace. After a long exchange of pleasantries, we got down to business.

"So, where do we go first?" I asked, figuring we'd hit the road running.

He looked at me blankly. "I don't know," he replied with a shrug. "Don't you know?"

I took this as a sign of things to come.

We hailed a taxi and sped through the holy chaos of Mexico City's rush hour with its oppressive humidity, din of honking traffic, and aroma of meat tacos and tailpipe exhaust. Next to me, Jesús frantically worked two cell phones to set up the first interviews. I'd hoped to spend the first week of my stay in Mexico talking with experts. But now, watching Jesús, I assumed I'd spend the first few days aimlessly touring the city.

THE SUN BONUS

But I'd underestimated Jesús. By the next morning, he'd arranged appointments with most of the people on my list. We headed first to a think tank, the Latin American Faculty of Social Sciences (FLACSO), located on a peaceful, leafy campus on the edge of the city. There we looked up a political scientist named Benjamin Temkin, who had taped a note on his office door with a quote from W. C. Fields: "I am free of all prejudice. I hate everyone equally."

A middle-aged academic in a tweed jacket with a fringe of brown hair on his balding dome, Temkin greeted us with

Mexico Facts

Region: North America

Location: Bordered by the United States, Gulf of Mexico, and the Caribbean Sea, Belize, and Guatemala.

Population: 109.6 million people

a smile. Just before we arrived, he'd been working on a spreadsheet of data from the World Values Survey, the World Health Organization, and Latinobarómetro, a Chile-based periodical study of attitudes toward democracy, trust, and other issues pertaining to Latin America. "I love spreadsheets," he said when he caught me looking over his shoulder at his screen. As an exercise, he'd been comparing the average annual temperatures in 40 capital cities around the world with the suicide rates in each country (the latter is a factor generally thought to be inversely related to happiness). It was a clever idea. His analysis clearly showed that the colder the climate, the higher the suicide rate, with Lithuania topping the list with 31 suicides per 1,000 people, and Mexico at the bottom with only 4 suicides per 1,000 people. You might conclude from this that the colder the country, the more people kill themselves, he said. (Perhaps

The Sun Bonus

Being happy can be as simple as stepping outside on a sunny day. The sun provides us with vitamin D, also known as the "happiness vitamin," which naturally increases the levels of the feel-good chemical serotonin in the brain. Doctors often prescribe sunlight to their patients who suffer from seasonal depression during the winter months.

the additional hours of darkness are depressing.) But it would be premature to do that, he warned.

"What we can conclude with certainty is that Mexico and indeed all countries near the Equator enjoy something we could call the sun bonus," he said. "All things being equal, places with sunnier weather are slightly happier than their northern cousins." This was important to understanding Mexican happiness, he said. By most measures Mexicans should be rather unhappy. On the world ranking of the Human Development Index (HDI), a widely accepted measure of "objective" well-being that takes into account the levels of income, education, and health care, Mexico ranks somewhere in the middle at 53rd. That's because about 60 percent of its population are poor and about 20 percent live in conditions of extreme poverty, and, as the index generated by the World Value Surveys suggests, on the average, richer, healthier, more highly educated people tend to be happier.

But not so with Mexico.

When it comes to happiness, Mexico ranks *second* in the World Values Survey, well ahead of the United States, western Europe, and other developed nations! Mexicans, in other words, seem to have developed a secret sauce that makes them happy, despite the drawback of, well, living in Mexico. "There's a lot more happiness here than the 'objective' standard of living would suggest," Temkin said.

According to some experts, a family of four in Mexico needs only about $320 per month to satisfy its basic needs. Below that income level, people really suffer. Above that, more money does not buy much more happiness. In the United States, on the other hand, a household would need $5,000 per month to optimize income and happiness. That makes it look as if Mexico has "bought" its current level of happiness for a bargain price.

"Of course the danger of this information is that politicians may interpret it to mean that they can say to poor people, 'Okay, you don't have education, health, or decent employment, but you're happier than people in other countries, so don't make trouble,'" he said. Temkin stressed that the fact remains that a decent level of health, education, and income constitutes a basic right of people and is necessary to sustain both objective and subjective well-being.

"Can you tell me why?" I asked.

"Isn't that your job to find out?"

THE MEXICAN X-FACTOR
Jesús and I spent most of the next two days trying to get a better sense of Mexico's recipe for happiness. A few of the ingredients that I had assumed were prerequisites for happiness—a trustworthy government, good health care, and a decent income—barely figured into the mix here. Sure, we might be able to attribute a small portion of Mexico's sunny outlook to the sun itself. But then Haiti and Sierra Leone are sunny, too, and they rank among the world's least happy places. Something else is going on.

To find out what that might be, I met a political scientist named Miguel Basáñez for lunch in a Parisian-like café.

Mexico: The Secret Sauce of Happiness

Basáñez had suggested we meet at 2:30, which seemed kind of late for a midday meal. But the trendy Rojo Bistro was buzzing with the clinking of silverware, the staccato drone of business conversations, and the occasional burst of laughter from a table of smartly dressed young women. Basáñez, with slicked-back gray hair and an aristocratic mustache, was wearing a charcoal suit with a Montblanc pen in his shirt pocket when he showed up late. "I'm sure you're familiar with the Latin sense of punctuality," he said wryly as he sat down.

Educated at the London School of Economics, Basáñez saw Mexico's happiness as a product of both its culture and its recent history. For much of the 20th century, one political party—the Institutional Revolutionary Party (PRI)—ruled Mexico. The PRI, launched in the aftermath of the Mexican Revolution to champion the rural and farming populations, soon had become the political machine of leaders who proved to be neither by nor for the people. Holding tightly to the reins of power for decades, PRI leaders repressed dissent. In 1968, under the PRI's watch, Mexican police massacred several hundred people, including students who were protesting the policies of President Gustavo Díaz Ordaz. When the PRI finally lost the presidency in the 2000 elections, a sense of relief washed over the nation. The Mexican people had finally gained the right to say who governed them. And with that came a spike in happiness.

During the heyday of the PRI, Mexicans had struck a Faustian bargain, Basáñez said. The people agreed to put up with one-party regime in exchange for a half century of meteoric growth, during which Mexico transformed itself from a rural to an urban society. But after a catastrophic earthquake hit Mexico City, the peso was devalued, and banks were nationalized, the economic crisis came to a head in the mid-1990s. Only when Mexicans felt a surge in freedom in 2000 did a surge of enthusiasm occur, aided by the NAFTA free trade agreement that gave a boost to the economy again.

"So you think that freedom explains why Mexico is experiencing higher levels of happiness?" I asked.

"Yes and no," he replied. "Humans have a complex relationship with freedom."

Most happiness experts agree, said Basáñez, that for a society to flourish, certain conditions have to be met—a decent economy, basic social stability, and so on. In most countries, economic freedom seems to go hand in hand with happiness: Societies thrive when their people can easily start businesses, get loans, and let their ingenuity and hard work breed success. Political freedom does not seem to matter as much; countries where people report high levels of well-being are not necessarily places where people are free to organize, to vote, and to provide input on how they're governed.

This is not the case for Mexico, Basáñez said.

The number of Mexicans who say they feel free has soared since the PRI lost its 80-year stranglehold on the presidency. "It turns out that despite its low impact on happiness elsewhere, political freedom is an important value for Mexicans, and they are experiencing more of it lately," he said.

Mexico: The Secret Sauce of Happiness

Basáñez thinks the Mexican X-factor—the secret sauce—probably has to do with disposition and an emphasis on social life over dedication to work. When he lived in New Jersey, Basáñez saw that people were in the office by 8 a.m. sharp, but when he tried to get co-workers out for socializing after work, they'd be too busy. Or he'd get them out but they were available only until 9 p.m. sharp, and they'd go home. "I could call 30 friends right now for a party at home, and most of them would come right away," said Basáñez. "We'd drink and laugh all night. And when we're done, we'd be hugging each other saying that we love each other. Of course, no one would be in the office tomorrow. The American system is good for productivity but not for the soul. The Mexican system is good for the soul but terrible for productivity." Indeed, a recent study carried out by Gallup-Healthways shows that social time massively affects day-to-day happiness. It suggests that for most people spending six to seven hours in social time each day helps to maximize their well-being. And full-time workers do best with about nine hours of social time to maximize their happiness—even more if their jobs are stressful.

"The secret," Basáñez concluded, "has to do with maintaining just the right tension between making a living and savoring life." By now our lunch had arrived: shrimp capellini and a Napa Valley chardonnay.

"Have you seen the surveys that show that the people of Monterrey are happier than anyone else in Mexico?" I asked. "Do you think it's true?"

"You know," he said, twirling pasta around his fork, "I never thought of it, but that sounds right. People in the north, in general, are better off than the rest of the country. They have better jobs, better health care, and better services. But remember, this is by Mexico's standards, not the United States'. Northerners have a reputation for working harder than those in the south. So, while they may have a Latin sense of time urgency, they still work hard enough to cover the basic standard requirements of happiness—food, shelter, health care, some education, and mobility—while enjoying life. They're also more candid and religious."

"Anything else?" I asked.

Basáñez put down his fork, sat back, and closed his eyes. "This is not unique to Monterrey," he replied after a long pause. "But Mexico has an amazing ability to laugh in the face of the hardship and thereby make it more tolerable. We laugh at sickness, poverty, and even death. We even have a holiday to celebrate death. November 2, the Day of the Dead, is one of the biggest holidays of the year."

LAUGH THERAPY

Okay, time for a reality check. Before we skip too far down the primrose lane of Mexican happiness, we should acknowledge a few of the more obvious potholes. Mexico has one of the highest disparities between rich and poor in the world, for example. In the United States, someone in the top ten percent income bracket makes ten times more money than someone in the lowest ten percent. In Mexico the wealthiest ten percent has more than twenty-five times the income of the poorest.

Then there's the question of crime, with hundreds of police murdered each year in ongoing drug wars and rampant kidnappings for ransom. The month I was there, two police chiefs in Nuevo León were assassinated, their bodyguard was handcuffed to a chain-link fence and shot in the head, and a journalist was seriously injured when gunmen stormed the newspaper's offices. And the drug cartels aren't the only problem. The World Values Survey shows a broad distrust of the police in the country. Fifty-five percent of Mexicans said their level of confidence in the government was "not very much" or "none at all," while their lack of confidence in the police was even higher, with about 66 percent responding negatively.

One woman told me a story about being robbed at gunpoint in a bookstore. "I didn't even report it," she said. "I knew that nothing would happen and I'd lose eight hours in the police station. Something like five percent of crimes are prosecuted. The police are abusive or inept." She went on to describe one of her family's long Sunday dinners (a concept known as *sobremesa*—lingering at the table over a meal), when they discussed crime for the entire meal. "Everyone has their tale of robbery, housebreaking, or mugging," she said.

How do Mexicans cope? A popular joke suggests a clue: A contest was held to find the most effective police force in the world. The test consisted of letting a rabbit run free in the woods and seeing which police force could find the rabbit fastest. It took the FBI three hours to find their rabbit, the German police found theirs in two, and Scotland Yard took only 90 minutes. After five hours, the Mexican police force hadn't found their rabbit. An hour later, the Mexicans showed up pulling a weeping and terrified elephant. The judges pointed out to the Mexican police that this animal was not a rabbit. The elephant, overhearing this, immediately fell to its knees and said, "I swear I am a rabbit, just don't hit me anymore!"

To get a better feeling for Mexican humor and its role in the nation's happiness recipe, I tracked down Mexico's most popular clown, a TV personality named Victor Trujillo. Known to millions as Brozo the Creepy Clown, Trujillo had donned a green wig and red nose every morning for almost a decade to deliver his mix of obscene humor, news, and political commentary on a show called *El Mañanero* (a double entendre meaning "morning quickie"). When I caught up with him at the Univision studios in Mexico City, Trujillo broke out of a production meeting that looked more like a bunch of drinking

Best Medicine

Researchers at California State University studied the link between humor and life satisfaction by bringing happiness and humor programming to senior citizens. Those who participated in the programming, which included interactive activities and joke telling, showed significant increases in self-reported life satisfaction.

buddies telling jokes and led me into his small office. There, a huge, $75,000 fine art print of a winged child, from Gregory Colbert's "Ashes and Snow" exhibit, hung over a neat, contemporary glass-topped desk and a new Apple computer— not the decor of your usual clown. Indeed, I knew from my research that Trujillo's methods contained a certain genius. He once prompted a corrupt city official to resign on live national TV by playing a secretly taped video of the guy stuffing a $45,000 bribe into his briefcase. Snickering under his green wig and red nose, Trujillo asked the official, "Can you comment on this video?"

"Mexican humor is like laugh therapy on a national scale," Trujillo told me after we'd settled into our conversation. We'd been talking about the corruption in the police force. "You Americans can believe in your police, we can't. Here they just add to misery." Trujillo is a big man with a shaved head and rimless glasses. This morning, instead of his clown suit, he was wearing a kelly green warm-up suit, New Balance sneakers, and two USB drives around his neck.

"In Mexico, humor is not a vehicle to poke fun at people as it often is in other countries," he explained. "We don't laugh at the Indians, or the blacks, or the gays. Here it's something to give us space and time before we just get mad. We don't have much power, so we laugh at those who do. It's a balm against pain." As he talked, he gesticulated excitedly, stretching his arms grandly to make a point. Ridiculing those in power helps society to cope.

"It does no good to cry, so we laugh," he said.

MEXICO'S POCKET OF HAPPINESS

Over the next week, Jesús and I met with economists, social scientists, and an anthropologist. I learned that, statistically speaking, freedom of choice is the single biggest predictor of happiness—as well as a few roots of Mexican happiness that would make sense to me later. We decided it was time to fly to Monterrey and meet some of Mexico's happiest people. When I met him in the hotel lobby to leave for the airport, he was garbed in the kind of rhinestone-studded T-shirt favored by L.A. rock bands.

"You can forget about sleep for the next couple of days," he warned.

As our plane rose out of the rust-colored smog of Mexico City and headed north, the scene below looked like a giant transistor board—a wild circuitry of *avenidas* and *calles* etched between seemingly endless low, cinder-block housing. About a hundred miles north into the trip, the urban snarl finally thinned and gave way to a patchwork of parched terrain hinting at agricultural activity.

The flight took us past the jagged peaks of the Sierra Madre Oriental to the foothills near Monterrey, a smaller, less chaotic version of Mexico City. Like its bigger cousin, Monterrey looks chaotic, as if urban planning hadn't suggested itself to the city's founders. Streets radiate from the central square like cracks in a window shattered by a hurled rock. Flanked by the green tufts of parks and playgrounds, the Santa Catarina River loops through town. La Huasteca, a miniature mountain range that looks like an enormous, crescent-shaped Bundt cake, hems the city to the west. To the east, houses thin out to scrubby desert and dusty ranchland. With a population of 1.1 million in Monterrey proper and a few million more spread around its suburbs, the metropolitan area is big enough to afford good schools, good parks, and other basic infrastructure without devolving into the crush that is Mexico City. In many respects, it looks more like Laredo, Texas, just two hours to the north by car.

History, it appears, favored Monterrey. The states of Nuevo León and Coahuila have long been among Mexico's most prosperous. The confluence of European settlers, local skills, rural grit, and proximity to the United States has paid off. The area's per capita income of $14,000 is one of the highest in the country. When it comes to work and making money, the region seems to have found a sweet spot: tapping economic success without going overboard in pursuit of wealth. Monterrey's city motto, "Work tempers the spirit," supremely sums up this attitude.

One might trace the roots of the region's economic success all the way back to conquistador Hernán Cortés. After he sacked the Aztecs in the 16th century he awarded land in the north to a band of his men, many of them Jewish, and an allied group of Tlaxcala Indians. At first, the hot, barren landscape may have seemed like a booby prize, a place of cactus and rock with slim potential. But an independent-minded culture took root here, and it turned out to be more diverse and entrepreneurial than those in other parts of the conquered lands. Over the centuries, the region continued to attract immigrants, who built an economy based on cattle and cotton. The area's unique culture combined indigenous recipes and Jewish influences like *samita,* a bread baked with cheese, raisins, peanuts, and sugar; floral blouses and wide-brimmed hats; and polka bands alongside mariachis. Today, almost everyone here is a mestizo, of mixed heritage, with perhaps more European influences than indigenous ones. You'll find plenty of locals with surnames like Valdez and Rodriguez, but the Muellers and Cohens remain part of the mosaic too.

Nuevo León is also home to thriving steel, glass, cement, refining, and brewing industries, the latter an outgrowth of German settlement in the area. Eighty-six percent of the land is used for raising livestock, while petrodollars have accelerated the region's affluence. According to the Human Development Index, the state ranks highest in all of Mexico due to its strong economic climate and sophisticated hospitals, schools, universities, and infrastructure. But, as I learned during my first week in the area, this strong economy probably does little to explain the region's outsize happiness.

SMALL DIFFERENCES, BIG RESULT

"Family, health, and faith in God: These are what count most to people here," said Nicole Fuentes, an economist at the University of Monterrey. The university, a cluster of modern buildings surrounded by green, manicured grounds, contrasts starkly with the prickly brown Sierra Madre foothills. We were sitting in the school's cafeteria, surrounded by hundreds of casually dressed (think Gap apparel) students who would have looked right at home in any community college in South Texas. Fuentes herself was wearing blue jeans, Nike running shoes, and a white maternity blouse that was doing its seam-bursting best to cover her soon-to-be-born daughter.

A graduate of Columbia University, Fuentes had landed in Monterrey to study, of all things, happiness. As a student, she became interested in using the tools of economics—data and analysis—to understand what brings people satisfaction in life. She had questioned the generally accepted rules that well-being increases with happiness and that gross national product is the best measure of national happiness. In general, when you plot per capita income against happiness levels, you get an upward-sloping line that levels off at a certain income. As income goes up (to a certain point), so should happiness. But that's not what you see in Monterrey. There the data form a flat scatter plot, more like a cloud of dots. In other words, something else influences happiness there more than income does.

So if rising income didn't create more happiness, she wanted to know, what did? Fuentes ticked off a long list of objective measures of happiness—things that you can easily measure:

- **Better education**—Two of the best private universities in the country are located here: the Monterrey Institute of Technology and the University of Monterrey. Many private schools are bilingual. Teachers speak to students in English from nursery school on up.

- **Better medical services**—A higher percentage of people have access to hospitals and medical care in Monterrey compared to other Mexican cities.

- **Geography**—Monterrey is close to the United States. Proximity to goods and services favors people here.

- **Better government**—Since the 1960s, Monterrey has had two strong political parties that alternate power (the region was the first to elect a mayor from the party that opposes the PRI). This translates into more competition and less corruption.

- **Better infrastructure**—Bigger and better streets, an international airport, a subway line, lots of public parks, two football stadiums, and one arena.

As part of her research into happiness factors—the ones that people themselves report—Fuentes listened to residents of Monterrey. In late 2002, she and her team mapped out 80 blocks of the metropolitan area and polled hundreds of people to find out what they valued in their lives. After conducting some 574 interviews about domains of life, Fuentes found that three out of four people considered themselves happy—an extraordinary proportion. When it came to money, she found that for a family of four, any income above $4,000 a year brought *no additional happiness*. In fact, income ranked so far down the list of values cited by residents that it was considered "trivial"—especially among the poorest people. Even 44 percent of the people who said they were dissatisfied with their economic situation still said they were happy overall with their lives. So, if these people in the happiest region of the happiest country in the Western Hemisphere believed that money played almost no role in their happiness, what did?

"We found that about 80 percent of the people we polled believed in God and that people who went to church at least once a week—about half of respondents—were the happiest," Fuentes said. Indeed, worldwide research shows that religious people are happier than nonreligious ones. But in Mexico there are more happy religious people than there are elsewhere.

Family was also a factor, Fuentes said. Married people were most likely to be happy. Conversely, the least happy were men who had been widowed and women who were divorced. Her research mirrored that of a European study in which subjects were outfitted with a PDA that pinged them randomly and asked them to report their mood. The study showed that they were in the most positive mood when they were with family, followed by being with friends, and finally being alone. Beyond marriage, it was the expansive sense of family that seemed to explain an additional happiness boost, she said.

Fuentes herself grew up in the town of Puebla, south of Mexico City. She moved to Monterrey in 1998 after marrying a local lawyer. The two towns are about the same size, but Fuentes notes a long list of contrasts that help explain why Monterrey seems to have an edge over Puebla. The cultural life of Monterrey is richer, with more art galleries and theaters, she said. The International Forum of Cultures attracts new art and ideas to the region. Monterrey invests deeply in public spaces, such as playgrounds. Walkways and bike lanes line major streets, making exercise easier. Fuentes specifically mentioned Paseo de Santa Lucia, which resembles San Antonio's River Walk. "These places are great because they are attractive, open to everyone, and you don't need to spend time or a lot of money to enjoy them," she said.

But what struck her as well were the small differences in daily life that add up to something important. When she first moved to Monterrey, Fuentes said, it was okay to leave your door unlocked at night, to drive with your car windows down, or to take a walk alone at night—a level of security, she said, many people in Mexico did not enjoy. (Sadly, neither do people in Monterrey today, given its recent epidemic of crime.) Local investment in parks and recreational trails continues to mean that people—regardless of income—can enjoy the outdoors with their families. When Fuentes heard from friends in Puebla, by contrast, they often complained that the only place to take kids is the shopping mall. She noted a certain civic pride in Monterrey. For instance, in the holiday season, streets are decorated and holiday parades are held for children.

"I was impressed the first time I went to the soccer stadium here," said Fuentes. "Fans danced and sang the whole 90 minutes of the match. Nonstop." (This observation made sense to me, especially in light of the local enthusiasm for religion. As anyone who's ever been to northern Mexico knows, soccer is just another form of religion.) Finally, she said, people here are hard workers: "They work hard enough to get everything done, but not too hard that they miss the important things."

A REAL PANACEA

Of the many insights into Mexican happiness that Fuentes offered from her research, the two that interested me most involved faith and family. On the surface, both factors seemed obvious, so I wondered if there was something different about Monterrey's brand of the two. We know that religious people are happier than nonreligious people, but does religion have a stronger impact in this area of the world? As for family, it's no surprise that we will all be happier if we're in a good relationship with our spouse, are close to our kids, and love our parents. But are Monterrey families different from families elsewhere? Is there something about them that could teach us how to think differently about our own families and how to spend our own time and resources?

One Friday afternoon, I visited one of the neighborhoods where Nicole had done her research, a working-class enclave called Santa Catarina in the shadow of the mountains of La Huasteca. I walked up and down the largely quiet streets of two-story homes painted pastel pinks, greens, and blues, with tall wooden doors and ornate iron-grated windows. Majestic Monterrey oaks arched overhead, their leaves filtering the heat of a withering midday sun. The streets were quiet with the serenity of the afternoon siesta, but in front of one house, I found three women sitting on cement blocks and chatting energetically.

"*Buenos días,*" I said, and introduced myself. (I'm six feet three and speak Spanish with a powerful Minnesota accent, so that phrases like *por supuesto*—"of course"—sound disquietingly like "Ya, you betcha.") "I'm writing a book about happiness," I blurted. "Do you mind if I talk to you?"

The women looked up at me with an expression of terror. Or maybe disdain. But a moment later, Silva Idalia, a 60-something grandma wearing cutoff jeans and a pink T-shirt, nodded in acquiescence. She introduced me to the other women, Mari Castro and Christina Zavala, and told me that they were neighbors and friends. As we talked, their six school-age kids squealed with delight as they kicked a half-inflated soccer ball up and down the street.

The three women met here every day after the midday meal, Silvia said. Their husbands, like most men in the

Gathering Joy

Nobel laureate Daniel Kahneman developed the "day reconstruction method" to measure people's happiness during each part of the day. This unique way of reporting happiness, in segments rather than as a collective whole, showed that the least happy time of the day was when people were alone (commuting to work or school) and the happiest portions were with others (dinner with family or interacting with friends).

neighborhood, earned modest incomes, perhaps $500 per month, to support multigenerational households of seven to twelve people. The women stayed home, took care of children, cleaned, and made the meals. During the warm hours of mid-afternoon, they got together to gossip and to comment on the state of the world. Christina, in her late 20s, lived with five adults, including her mother-in-law, an 8-month-old baby, and a pair of 11-year-old cousins who helped her with chores. She went to church every Sunday. Once a year, on April 11, the anniversary of her grandmother's death, about 60 members of her extended family got together for a picnic at the grave.

"And do you know all 60 of those people?" I asked.

"Of course," she said. "They are my family."

When I asked the women if they were happy, they shrugged and looked at one another. "Yes, we're happy," Silvia said, breaking the silence. "We could all use a little more money, but we have what we need, and what we don't have God takes care of."

"What would you do if you had more money?"

"Probably buy bigger houses," Christina said. "But on the other hand, we probably wouldn't meet like this every afternoon. So, maybe not."

It occurred to me that if they were better off and could afford to live in one of the many new cul-de-sac developments going up on the edge of Monterrey, where houses are separated by wide lawns, these women wouldn't see each other as often. Here, in this neighborhood of shared challenges and easy camaraderie, all that is needed for a pleasant afternoon are three cinder blocks and a limp soccer ball.

Leaving the women to continue their chatting, I wandered on down the street. For the rest of the afternoon, I took an informal poll on happiness with everyone I encountered—three teenagers sitting outside a small grocery store, a woman sweeping her sidewalk, a street vendor. None were too surprised to hear that other people in the neighborhood said they were happy. "People know each other here," said the woman with the broom.

Late that afternoon, I noticed a group of five women carrying an appliance-size clear plastic box containing a statue of Jesus, his bloody heart wrapped in a barbwire of thorns. They were heading to their weekly prayer meeting at the house of a friend. Inside were gathered about 20 women, ranging from 20 to 70 years old, to say the Rosary in a cramped, cement-walled, tiled-floor living room that was cooled only by a rotating fan. They were gathering this week to pray for a friend who had just been diagnosed with cancer. It was a quiet, serious affair that made me feel like an intruder. When I asked the woman next to me if she knew the women for whom we were praying, she shook her head no and shushed me.

Following the prayers, the gathering segued into a social occasion, where the rosary beads went into purses and Coca-Colas came out of the refrigerator. Prayer turned to easy gossip. The young woman who had cut me off during the prayers came up to me to apologize. "I come here every Friday because I know if I get sick, this group will pray for me," she said. "It gives me comfort."

Her comment reflects a common theme in surveys of Mexicans. Like people in the United States, Mexicans express a near-universal belief in God (95 percent in the United States and 98 percent in Mexico). But when asked, "How important is God in your life?" more than 80 percent of Mexicans responded with a 10 on a scale of 1 to 10—compared with only 58 percent in the United States. Nearly 59 percent of Mexican respondents, moreover, said religion is "very important" in their lives—compared to 47 percent in the United States. In Nuevo León, the numbers are even more extreme. Here, in addition to traditional Catholicism, people practice a more potent blend of European and homegrown beliefs that taps into cultural traditions dating back to the time of the Aztecs.

This spiritual blend is vividly illustrated by a cult surrounding José "El Niño" Fidencio, a clubfooted child who was believed to have a knack for the supernatural. In 1906, at the age of eight, he reportedly laid his hands on his mother's

Faith and Happiness

Religion and faith are often linked to happier lives. However, according to Ed Diener, author of the book *Happiness,* it's religion's broader lessons that lead to happiness—acting selflessly and morally, having a sense of purpose, finding meaning in daily activities, and expanding positive emotions on a continual basis.

broken arm and the arm instantly healed. He then started using prayers, touch, and herbal medicine to cure people of everything from colds to muteness. By the time he was a young man living in the town of Espinazo, his reputation had spread across Mexico. In 1928, Mexico's president (whose earlier campaign to suppress the Catholic priesthood almost got Fidencio arrested) sought El Niño's help for a skin condition. The boy famously snubbed the president before eventually seeing him. After he cured the ailing politician, thousands of hopeful people descended on Espinazo. By the time of his death in 1938, El Niño had become the most famous *curandero* in Mexico. Even today, 80 years after his death, tens of thousands of visitors still descend upon Espinazo each year to remember him and to seek cures for just about everything that modern medicine can't address or that meager incomes won't cover.

In another tumbleweed desert town 50 miles northwest of Monterrey, I met El Niño's modern counterpart, a diminutive 15-year-old girl named Adriana Pérez Alaya. Known simply as La Niña, Alaya has also gained an international reputation as a child healer. Five years ago, as the story goes, Alaya met an old woman on her way to church. They exchanged a greeting, during which time the woman told Alaya that she was suffering from stomach cancer and was going to die soon. The ten-year-old simply put her hands on the woman and said, "You're cured." The woman went home, and soon thereafter her stomach cancer was said to have disappeared. News spread quickly throughout Nuevo León. Soon other sick people started showing up at Alaya's door and camping out-side her bedroom window. The demure child, whose parents had instilled in her a respect for elders, dutifully put her hands on the strangers, murmured a small prayer of her own inven-tion, and sent them on their way.

Within a year, dozens of miracle seekers were showing up in Paredón every day. They'd camp out under the fourth grad-er's bedroom and mob her on her way to school. Then they'd wait for her outside the school. Adriana's parents tried to pro-tect her by serving as her bodyguards. But they were sim-ple farmers, out of their league. Finally they took her out of school, turned an adjacent lot into an ad hoc clinic, walled off their compound, and cloistered their daughter.

The day I visited her, about 200 people had made the pil-grimage to see La Niña. The lime green walls of her family's home were plastered with letters and photos of followers who had visited her, as well as newspaper clippings attest-ing to her miracles. There was a note in crayon from a nine-year-old girl who said she'd been cured of cancer. A typed letter from a man who said he'd been relieved of bone pain. A lock of hair Scotch-taped to a letter from a man thanking La Niña for curing his baldness. Inside, patients with every-thing from rheumatism to cancer waited to see La Niña. They had swollen limbs, diabetes, high blood pressure, and other ailments. Looking bone-tired, two leathery-skinned cowboys in white hats and boots slouched on a bench. But when one of La Niña's many assistants (all of whom wore white trousers and a rosary slung over a purple shirt) led a song praising El Niño Fidencio and La Niña, the cowboys sat up and sang.

Claudia Ortiz, a heavy 34-year-old woman, told me she'd been trying to conceive a child for three years. She'd spent her life's savings on fertility treatments but had had no success. Six months earlier, she'd started visiting La Niña. Each time, the teenager had put her hand over Claudia's uterus and whispered a blessing. During the third visit, La Niña said she felt the presence of a baby. Today, Claudia had brought along an ultrasound image. She held it up to the sun and pointed to a tiny fetus situated above her hips. Weeping, she told me, "This is my son. I have La Niña to thank."

Roberto Rosco had broken both of his legs six months earlier, when he had fallen into a well. Doctors screwed in a plate, but the bone couldn't take it. Facing a lifetime in a wheelchair, Rosco had started visiting La Niña. "Every time I come, I feel better," he told me. "My bones are stronger."

Later I met Dr. Maria Suarez, a former family practitioner from Monterrey, who suffers from epilepsy. She started coming to La Niña six mouths ago, after giving up on clinically prescribed remedies. "My faith in her is the only thing that relieves my suffering," she said.

"But you're a trained physician," I replied. "Do you really believe in her powers?"

"Absolutely," she said.

Despite the long line of people waiting to see La Niña, I was invited inside. I took a seat by the wall to watch. A short, attractive teenager, she stood before an altar cluttered with images of Jesus Christ, the Virgin of Guadalupe, the Buddha, and El Niño Fidencio. It was cool and dark, save for the sifted light from an opaque window and half a dozen candles. La Niña wore white trousers and a white T-shirt draped with a purple satin cape. Her face was framed by long, black hair pulled back in a ponytail. Her unblinking eyes slanted upward.

A mother wheeled her young son into the sacristy. He was bald except for a few wisps of hair—presumably as a result of cancer treatments—and he sat listlessly in his chair. La Niña stared at him for a long diagnostic moment. Then she grabbed a bedsheet and covered him. She took up a bouquet of laurel boughs and whisked it over the boy with fluid, curlicue motions as she chanted a prayer. Then she whipped off the sheet, gave it to the boy's mother, and told her that her son's cure would come if she covered the boy up with the sheet every day for the next month.

I watched several more patients come and go. Finally, the *curandera* looked at me and whispered to an assistant. "La Niña would like to bless you," the assistant said. I figured, what the hell?

I approached the altar and stood facing her. She was just over half my height. She held my hands in hers and looked up at me. Her forehead was smooth, her cheeks glistened with sweat. Her eyes, which were at half-mast, looked right through me, yet with a certain tenderness. She was attractive, but in a genderless way. She inspired the sort of affection one might feel for an infant. La Niña waved her hand up and down my torso, murmured a blessing, and captivated me. I felt a sort of hypnotic lull, a creeping belief that this kid had powers. Then she opened her eyes and told me I was done. What? Already?

An hour later, I was back in the waiting area. Another assistant came out and told me that La Niña's family would like to invite me to lunch. I felt strangely guilty striding past all of the sick and needy people as I headed into the prophet's inner sanctum. Inside, behind the altar, was the house where La Niña lived with her mom, dad, brothers, and sisters. The kitchen was full of people, dozens of assistants dressed in purple, either preparing or eating lunch. Adriana's father sat at a table. He wore a cowboy hat and a denim shirt. He looked exhausted and somewhat neglected. I sat down next to him and was served beans, sweetened bread, and tortillas.

He told me how hard it was to be a simple farmer and the father of a prophet at the same time. "To come home from the fields to see hundreds of people lined up to be healed by my nine-year-old daughter was hard to take. Five years ago, I had to build a house around Adriana's healing powers," he said.

Moments later, La Niña herself came in and took a seat next to me. She was served a plate of food. Now she wasn't the miracle-working healer with scores of people waiting for five minutes of her time, but a kid at a lunch table drinking a Coke. After a long moment, I broke the silence by asking her if she remembered her first patient. She shook her head no. Then I asked how she healed.

"I don't really know," she replied. "I cure people with their own faith. I just help them find it." We fell quiet for a moment.

"What are you writing about?" she asked me suddenly, looking over my notebook and leaning an elbow on my knee. There was a residual power to her touch. "Happiness," I said. "Are you happy?"

"Yes, very happy," she replied. She was looking up at me searchingly with those timeless, faraway eyes. Then, suddenly, she was up. She walked over to her father and hugged and kissed him on the cheek. And then she was gone, back to the sick and the suffering.

I left Paredón wondering if Alaya's powers were nothing more than hocus-pocus, the same sort of empty faith healing you sometimes see at religious revivals. Or did La Niña possess something special, some culture-specific ability to stimulate an internal healing mechanism? Whatever the answer, an extraordinary number of people in this region turn to La Niña—and faith healers like her—in times of need. She addresses their pain and dispenses hope, the poor man's most valuable commodity. People leave feeling that they've been heard, that someone cared, if only for just a few minutes. For her followers—the poor and uninsured—La Niña provides a powerful dose of pain mitigation. And, as novelist Carlos Fuentes once said of his native country, it is impossible to understand Mexico without appreciating what it is to believe in miracles.

THE WISE MAN

The city of Saltillo lies 50 miles southwest of Monterrey in the Chihuahuan Desert. A cool, sunny, high-altitude oasis, Saltillo was recently voted "best city to live in" by a leading

Mexican business journal because of its colonial architecture, celebrated bird and desert museums, and *norteño* cuisine. Its population of half a million or so enjoys one of the nation's highest per capita incomes—about $14,000 per year.

I'd come to Saltillo to meet a newspaper columnist and humorist named Armando Fuentes Aguirre, who also goes by the name "El Catón" (the Wise Man). I'd been hearing about him since I arrived in Mexico City, where he is well known—even among serious academics—as a man who profoundly understands the soul of northeastern Mexico. Trained as a lawyer and experienced in teaching, Fuentes had spent more than four decades penning four columns daily for the 150 newspapers that published his work. A man who had traveled the world, had met Ronald Reagan, and had received dozens of awards for his writing, he is arguably the most famous chronicler of Mexico's daily life. But, more than that, he is famously happy.

I met Fuentes in Saltillo one Saturday morning at a brick-walled restaurant decorated with Aztec pottery and Toulouse-Lautrec posters. Outside, palm trees rustled in a warm, dry breeze. The town's mayor had gone to considerable trouble to arrange my meeting with El Catón, who was still a busy man at 68. When we finally sat down over tortillas, black beans, and eggs, he began the interview by thanking *me* for my time. He exuded a take-all-the-time-you-need attitude. He wore a corduroy sports jacket over a plaid shirt. His gray hair was tossed to one side, and his lantern jaw and steel-rimmed glasses might have been jarring on another man, but actually enhanced his pleasant demeanor.

Mexico: The Secret Sauce of Happiness

I liked him instantly.

"Did you know that all the worldwide databases point to this region as the happiest in the hemisphere?" I asked. "Do you have any idea why?"

"I'm not surprised," he replied. "They say that St. Peter is always a bit nervous when someone from Saltillo appears at the Pearly Gates."

"Why's that?"

"Because he knows that heaven is a downgrade from Saltillo."

He laughed and then turned professorial. "We've been isolated in this part of the country since the 16th century, surrounded by desert," he said. "We've had to be self-sufficient, to rely heavily on our neighbors and especially our families. We've had to work hard to survive, but that is tempered by the indigenous influence. Indians here in the north are the Chichimecas. Once a year, they have a huge party and drink *mitote* [a fermented corn beverage]. They drink until they fall to the ground. They dance, have sex, drink, and eat. When the Spanish friars came, they tried to convince the Chichimecas to give up the fiesta, and they justifiably refused. Why give up joy in your life with so much work to do? So we just incorporated it into our culture. We celebrate everything. Mother's Day. Father's Day. Godfather's Day. Saint's Days. Dead people's days. Something every week. We invent reasons together. We know how to mix work and pleasure."

El Catón looked at my empty coffee cup and called the waitress over to fill it. It was a sunny morning; rays of sunshine slanted through the window and spilled onto the table.

He rested his folded hands in front of him and looked at me through his glasses. As he waited for the next question, I noticed that his facial expression naturally settled into a smile.

"Can you talk more about faith and family?" I asked. "It seems you can't have a conversation about happiness in Mexico without those two topics coming up."

"Sure. You need to believe in something to be happy," he replied. "You need to believe in something bigger than yourself, something that transcends you. This gives you hope, and that is part of happiness. Your body needs company, but your soul needs company too. And that's the company of God. I think it's harder for an atheist to have company for the soul. We cannot live without faith, hope, and love. It's something we get from our elders. It's in everyone around us. If we live only for ourselves, we're not going to be happy.

"There's a story I tell to illustrate the Mexican notion of faith: Someone asks a farmer, 'What are you doing?'

"The farmer says, 'I'm plowing a field.'

"'Why are you plowing a field?'

"'To plant seeds.'

"'Why?'

"'To get wheat.'

"'Why?'

"'To make bread.'

"'Why?'

"'To live.'

"'Why?'

"'So I can plow a field.'

"Do you see the vicious cycle?" he asked. "But if you ask a child why she is picking a flower, she will say, 'To have something of beauty.'

"'Why?'

"'To make a bouquet.'

"'Why?'

"'To bring it to the Virgin.'

"Giovanni Papini actually wrote this," Fuentes said, referring to the early 20th-century Italian writer. "But it sums up the mind-set in this region too. If you think only about yourself, your problems will be endless—you'll have a new pain in your back, some part of your car will need fixing, your savings account won't be big enough. Fix one problem, and a new one always appears to take its place. But when you worry about someone else's problems, or volunteer your time, you take the light off of your own troubles. This is part of the reason I have a program where I feed about 100 kids every day."

I'd heard about Fuentes's quiet philanthropic work. While this region may be the happiest part of the Western Hemisphere, there continue to be pockets where people lack the basics. Potrero de Abrego, a village outside Saltillo is—or was—one such place. People there work for local landowners at poverty wages or scratch meager crops out of infertile soil. For a long time, many people went hungry. A few years ago, Fuentes noticed this, and it bothered him. He couldn't support the entire town, but he figured he could give the new generation a head start. So he and his wife started a program. They constructed a simple building, hired a dietitian to design a simple lunch that fulfilled kids' nutritional needs, and convinced mothers in the village to staff the place. Now, every day at noon, 107 children and 8 elderly people showed up for a daily meal. A dozen or so mothers volunteered to cook, serve, and clean up, and hence, once a day, much of the community came together. Since the program has been in place, children's math scores, science scores, and even athletic ability have surpassed all of the surrounding towns'— simply because of El Catón's meal-a-day generosity.

"We have so much, and they have almost nothing," he said of the villagers. "It's a way to say thank you. We don't want to get anything in return. It's not a huge act for a rich man."

A rich man? When I met him, Fuentes's income was likely no higher than that of a mid-level manager at an American corporation.

"We're not rich because we have a lot of money," he said. "We're rich because we have few needs. And we celebrate everything. In our family, if we don't have an occasion, we invent one. There are people who will never be happy because they want too much of life. If they don't get what they want, they don't let themselves be happy. The trick is to work for contentment. Then happiness will follow."

Fuentes left me with one last pearl of wisdom, his grandfather's recipe for happiness:

Drink without getting drunk
Love without suffering jealousy
Eat without overindulging
Never argue
And once in a while, with great discretion, misbehave.

Lessons from Mexico

Make no mistake, the people in and around Monterrey have serious problems. In many villages, kids suffer from malnutrition and lack of education. Talented, intelligent men and women are stuck working in breweries or factories that make jeans. Their dreams and aspirations are going unmet. The less fortunate feel they must leave their families and travel to the United States for work. Yet despite all these hurdles—the high levels of corruption and the relatively low levels of development and questionable governance—these Mexicans are blessed with, shall we say, happiness assets.

The Sun Bonus

Mexicans collect a small happiness bump from the sun bonus—more annual hours of sunlight than most of their neighbors to the north, and hence more vitamin D. There's more to this than sunny clichés may suggest. "Emerging research shows that tanning prompts manufacture of endorphins that give you a feeling similar to a runner's high," said Dr. Gregory Plotnikoff of the Allina Center for Health Care Innovation in Minneapolis. He also points to the importance of vitamin D for overall health, well-being, and longevity. "Safe sunning, no burning" means more health-promoting vitamin D —a compound many Americans lack in sufficient quantities.

A Personal Sense of Freedom

"The freer we feel, the happier we say we are," said Alejandro Moreno, a political scientist from the Mexico Autonomous Institute of Technology. "Statistically speaking, the sense of individual freedom of choice is, by far, the variable that contributes most significantly to happiness." Over the past 30 years, a growing sense of individual freedom has accompanied a growing sense of happiness. This isn't true of all countries (Singapore is one exception), but for Western societies that have been poor and repressed, policies that maximize freedom may boost well-being, too.

Nurturing Laughter

Mexican humor focuses not on an underclass or ethnicity, but on crooked cops, politicians on the take, and the difficult lives of everyday citizens. It serves as a stress-shedding device and a balm for the pain: Mexicans laugh at themselves, laugh at taxes, and quite literally laugh in the face of death.

But can the rest of us get happier by creating an environment of laughter? Nicole Fuentes believes so. "Humor and happiness are related in pretty much the same way that optimism and happiness are related," she says. "You can choose to be more optimistic, if you work at it. Humor leads to social bonding due to shared positive emotions and the discharge of negative ones." People who laugh more tend to be more extroverted, have higher levels of self-esteem, and lower levels of depression. Laughter has been associated with an array of health benefits—lowered stress levels and the release of beneficial hormones among them. "Laugh therapy" has become mainstream enough that the Pentagon has even paid some personnel to train in one version of it to help military families who are separated from loved ones. Mexicans in and around Monterrey are born into an environment of good humor. Perhaps it's a cue to spend more time watching the comedy channel and hanging out with jokers?

Just Enough Money

Norteños seem to have gotten it right when it comes to money, too. Consider the guitar as a metaphor. If the strings are too loose, the guitar plays flat; if the strings are too tight, it sounds sharp. The trick is to find just the right tension so the guitar is in tune. Mexicans, it seems, have an easier time getting their financial lives in tune. If you're an average Mexican, you're likely to be surrounded by people who are not running a status race. You feel less pressure to keep up with the proverbial Joneses except, perhaps, when it comes to socializing and party throwing. This environment of modest expectations enables people to feel good about themselves without competing for a big house, a fast car, or the latest fashions.

Faith Therapy

Then there's the *norteños'* special brand of religion. According to the General Social Survey, religious people tend to be happier than nonreligious people, even in the United States. But simply believing in God alone doesn't guarantee happiness. In countries such as Jordan and Algeria, more than 90 percent of people surveyed said religion was very important in their lives, yet these nations do not occupy the top rankings of subjective well-being. Somehow, the *norteños'* combination of indigenous influences meshed with Christian beliefs has yielded a more uplifting faith than that commonly found elsewhere. This supercharged faith helps people cope with hardship—even if it just means having someone listen to one's problems. It could also have something to do with the way that membership in a religious community boosts happiness. In any case, taking a cue from *norteños* and joining a faith-based community stacks the deck in favor of happiness. Religious communities that provide access to a built-in, social, weekly congregation offer a means for ritualized stress relief and self-assessment. (Research on the brain activity of Tibetan monks, for example, has shown that the more experienced practitioners of meditation have higher levels of activity in the left prefrontal cortex, the part of the brain where happiness "lives.") People who belong to a faith-based community are less likely to engage in risky behavior, and then there's the X-factor. If we pray for happiness, does it help us get happier? Most people in the world would say yes.

Oversocialize

Mexicans understand the importance of social interaction. They spend much of their day socializing with family and friends; a good party will almost always trump work. As you'll recall, psychologists have identified two types of happiness: *experienced* happiness and *remembered* happiness. We tend to remember high points and low points in our lives. But experienced happiness is the sum of the little joys throughout the day. You might not recall a drink with friends, a conversation over the fence, or happy hour with co-workers as highlights of your life, but working them in on a daily basis will increase your overall happiness. In this sense, *norteños* can offer a big lesson for overworked people living in other countries: Make friends and make time for them. Seven to nine hours of social time each day will likely maximize your happiness.

Family First

In Mexico, "family" is an expansive term that encompasses mom, dad, brothers, sisters, your grandma's sister's daughter, your uncle's neighbor, and your third cousin twice removed who is working in the United States. "Family and friends play a more central role in our lives than they do in most other countries," Fuentes said. "Both faith and family help create a social network that provides support in times of financial hardship or illness, and forms the basis of an informal economy that allows people to acquire goods and services they might not otherwise afford." Mexicans are able to tolerate a huge deal of problems and disorder in the environment, as long as the family is doing fine. Family is an invaluable source of support. Grandmothers take care of their grandchildren so that moms can go to work and earn money. The second generation takes care of their parents when they are old. In this regard, the lesson is clear: For most of us, the more time we spend with family and friends, the happier we'll be.

Counting Our Blessings

Perhaps the best advice, though, comes from Armando Fuentes Aguirre, the Wise One, who reminds us that 90 percent of happiness is the pursuit of simple *content-ment*—actively appreciating the good around us. The more we can take the focus off ourselves and forget our own problems, the happier we'll be.

CHAPTER FIVE

San Luis Obispo:
A Real American Dream

Making room for bikes is the only way to go in San Luis Obispo, California, a town that prides itself on making recreation and social interaction easier. Newer establishments often have a bike valet service. PHOTO BY DAN BUETTNER

San Luis Obispo:
A Real American Dream

Two and a half centuries ago, Father Junípero Serra, the Franciscan missionary, set out from San Diego on a journey up California's El Camino Real—the "King's Highway"— to a place the Spanish called the Bear Plain, where grizzlies were known to be abundant. There he told a small crew to build a church to spread Christianity among the Chumash people. Serra named the new mission after his favorite saint, Louis, bishop of Toulouse, which eventually lent its name to the town that grew up around the mission: San Luis Obispo.

This morning, I'm two miles away from that same church, with its austere whitewashed adobe walls, and I'm getting a history lesson from Kenneth Schwartz, professor emeritus of architecture at the nearby California Polytechnic State

University (Cal Poly). Schwartz designed and built the house we're sitting in—exactly the way he wanted it to be—and it's a testament to a life richly lived. There's African art on the walls. "I've visited all seven continents," he says as I admire one of the paintings. Shelves display framed photos of his children, grandchildren, and great-grandchildren in a living room surrounded by floor-to-ceiling windows with views of his well-manicured garden.

Schwartz is asking me to picture San Luis Obispo the way it looked in 1772, when it was still a Chumash hunting settlement. "Do you know the first thing the Spanish did when they started building a city in the New World?" he asks, narrowing his clear, blue eyes behind his glasses.

I shake my head.

He sticks his forefinger in his mouth, pops it out of his cheek, and holds it up in the air. Those blue eyes are laughing now. "They checked which way the wind blew," he says. That told them which way the street dust and animal dung would blow; they then skewed the directions of the streets so future buildings would block the winds from sweeping the streets. "Those early Spanish settlements in California were planned," he explains. "They followed the Law of the Indies, a dictate by King Philip of Spain set down in 1573." But in much of the United States, a different tradition took hold, and it strongly opposed this kind of didactic vision. "Our civic attitude has been, 'We're a democracy, dammit, and nobody is going to tell us what the hell to do with our land,'" Schwartz says. "It took a long time for this country to recognize that without some land-use regulations, there would just be chaos."

In 1952, when Schwartz moved from Los Angeles to teach at Cal Poly, he encountered this attitude among the town fathers of San Luis Obispo. At the time, the community had all the trappings of a postwar California boomtown, choked with neon signs and power lines, without any of the graceful towering trees that you see downtown today. Back then, according to Schwartz, San Luis Obispo was "Anyplace, U.S.A.," a nondescript western community of 14,000 controlled by a few powerful property owners and conservative business leaders. He decided to get involved in city government when a newly elected mayor offered him a seat on the city's planning commission. "Citizen planners were not experts in those days," he says. "They were the butcher, the baker, the candlestick maker." Besides, the planning commission's only power was as a recommending body, not as a decision-making body.

But in 1969, after eight years of planning, Schwartz decided to run for mayor and went on to become the longest serving mayor in the town's contemporary history, holding the office for five consecutive two-year terms until 1979. In fact, by the time Schwartz left office, the winds had changed, and San Luis Obispo had moved to the forefront of an American planning renaissance. The "reactionary business community," as he called it, that once ran the city council was replaced by a more progressive group of city leaders, who in turn set a new standard for signs, utility lines, and planted all those aforementioned trees. Under Schwartz, the downtown area became visually attractive and more pedestrian friendly. More important, Highway 101—the coastal freeway built on top of Father Serra's old Camino Real—no longer passed by the front of the mission and cut through the center of town. What used to be a central artery was completely blocked off to traffic, with a central mission plaza constructed in its place—kind of a central park running down to the banks of a cleaned-up San Luis Creek. Today there are walkways on either side of San Luis Creek, with terraced café patios across from the mission side filled with people trying out local wines or going for walks or checking out the art center or the historical museum on the edge of the plaza or the historic mission itself. The plaza has become the sparkling crown of what is now recognized as one of the happiest cities in the United States.

According a 2008 Gallup-Healthways study, in fact, the 44,000 residents of San Luis Obispo today enjoy stratospheric levels of emotional well-being. Not only are they more likely than residents of other U.S. cities to smile and to experience

San Luis Obispo Facts

Nation: United States of America

Location: Midway between Los Angeles and San Francisco on the Central Coast of California

City Population: 44,075 people

joy, they are also less likely to experience pain or depression. In fact, in terms of their overall emotional health, they ranked number 1 in the nation. People in San Luis Obispo are thriving with a sense of purpose, meaning that a majority of them expect things will get even better. And they are not only happy *in* their city, but also happy *with* their city—with much higher rates of satisfaction with their local government than citizens of other municipalities. So this begs the question: How did they do it? What can we learn from their experience? Can you actually plan a city to become one of the happiest in the United States?

THE MIDDLE KINGDOM

I'd come to San Luis Obispo to find answers to these important questions. Following a late-night, three-hour drive up the coast from Los Angeles, I found the small, family-run bed and breakfast called Petit Soleil—"little sun" in French—where I'd made a reservation. But by the time I arrived, the office had closed. Fortunately, I found an envelope taped to the outside of the door with my name on it. Inside were my room key and a note—"See you in the morning!"

The next day, after coffee and a quick breakfast, I inquired at the front desk about the nearest bicycle rental. John Conner, the impishly cheerful hotel owner (he owns the place with his wife, Dianne), was behind the desk. He brought me around front and unlocked one of the two house bikes, a sturdy chrome cruiser painted candy-apple red. I hopped on and was set to be on my way when I remembered—I still hadn't checked in!

"Can I give you my credit card?" I asked.

"Oh, let's just do it later," he said. "It's easier on my brain that way."

"But what if I just pedal off with your sweet bike and don't come back?" I asked.

"I trust you," he said, and beamed.

Both culturally and geographically, San Luis Obispo (or SLO as residents sometimes call it) is about halfway between Los Angeles and San Francisco. Dan Krieger, a Cal Poly professor who catalogs local color in his weekly history column in the *Tribune,* dubbed San Luis Obispo County the Middle Kingdom in his 1990 history. The San Luis Obispo region can almost claim its own castle—William Randolph Hearst built his walled fortress 45 minutes up the highway in San Simeon—but it's called the Middle Kingdom because it isn't in the orbit of either big city to the north or the south.

Riding through town on the main bike thoroughfare, the Bill Roalman Trail, you can look up and see one of the seven sisters—giant, grassy-tufted hills of volcanic rock—squatting just outside of town. There's an only-in-California, Dr.-Seuss-does-Swiss-chalet feel to the landscape here, with sea-foam green bosoms never quite out of your line of sight. In fact, the omnipresence of those hills makes you feel that, at any moment, you can just ride right out of town—and you really never are more than 20 minutes away from herb-blanketed mountain bike or hiking trails. On one hike, I freshened my breath with wild anisette plucked off the side of a trail leading up the tallest and most popular sister, Bishop's Peak. But don't get too lulled on the outskirts of this Whoville nestled into strange-looking mounds: There were signs warning "mountain lion habitat" on the entrance to a path behind the Poly campus. Mountain lions, five minutes from a Jamba Juice!

My favorite bike ride turned out to be zipping down the Monterey Street hill, right by the big Volvo dealership with its lot full of luxury convertibles, and right by the mission itself, to the farmer's market held every Thursday night, year-round. I parked my bike at the free "bike valet" (over 15,000 served). The kid put my bike behind velvet ropes (okay, maybe just ropes), gave me my ticket, and sent me down the street. It seemed like the entire town was at the farmer's market—middle-aged folks as well as the *Archie* set from campus—walking up and down Higuera Street hand in hand while using their free hands to squeeze cartoon-perfect tomatoes or to sample supermarket-shaming strawberries. The quality of this bounty of fresh produce was overwhelming to this Midwesterner, who was still getting over a long winter of trucked-in produce. Every possible type of bell pepper was on display, next to squash, citrus fruits, Japanese eggplant, pistachio butter, broccoli, and fiddlehead ferns, all of it perfect and produced locally.

And it wasn't just the diversity of the food that was on display: On one remarkable stretch of curb, the booth to the gay-lesbian alliance sat next to the libertarian booth, which was next to a population control booth, which was next to the California Highway Patrol booth (with two CHiPs standing out front in full khaki uniforms, complete with Ray-Ban aviators), which was next to the Nation of Islam booth and across the street from a dream interpretation tent. Smoke from a barbecued rib joint wafted over a vegan stand, and every time I walked by the Asian barbecue area they stopped chopping whatever they were chopping, smiled, and waved. Tolerant people appeared to be happy people.

As the Gallup-Healthways Well-Being Index had shown, the people of San Luis Obispo are mentally and physically healthy, ranking number 20 in the nation. They are also relatively wealthy. But a close look at these statistics also reveals that the people of San Luis Obispo are (to borrow Thomas Jefferson's enlightened turn of phrase) somehow more driven in the *pursuit* of happiness than people living elsewhere. Missions abound: There are more than 1,100 nonprofit organizations in San Luis Obispo County. Of 260,000 residents in the metropolitan area, more than 64,000 volunteer. And in a nation where, for better or for worse, the individual is more strongly identified with vocation than any other aspect of life, it's also significant that the citizens of SLO rank in the upper third for happiness at their jobs.

THE JOY OF WINE

Leslie Mead is one of those happy workers. Every morning, she commutes from her home in the Edna Valley past cow patches and vineyards, to her job at Talley Vineyards, a small winemaking operation in the Arroyo Grande Valley 6.8 miles away. "It's so beautiful," she said.

Before coming to SLO, Mead had lived in Santa Cruz, California, where she'd cared for her mother who was dying of cancer. Born in Virginia and raised in Honolulu, Mead had grown up a Navy brat, and as an adult she'd bounced around the West Coast—up to Oregon, down to Santa Cruz—working as a scuba diver in Hawaii then as an urban forester in Calaveras County. "I checked the trees around power lines," she said. Somehow, Mead had become a tree cop. She wasn't very happy.

Looking for a way to put her chemistry training to work (she'd studied chemistry in college and had loved its precision), she landed a gig at one of the largest vineyards in the country. Central California is one of the most picturesque places in the nation—when you can see it. Much of the time, it's blanketed by fog, and this was reflected in Mead's depressed mood. She liked her work at the winery, but she didn't like much else. The traffic during her commute was "intense," her neighborhood crowded and unfriendly, and everywhere she looked was another stinky, deadbeat, dreadlocked trustafarian with an outstretched palm. "The hippie

Great Grapes

Drinking even one glass of wine leads to increases in the happiness-inducing chemical dopamine in our brain. Enjoying that glass of wine with friends will also add to an enhanced feeling of cheer.

culture really bothered me," she says. "All these rich kids who thought it was cool to panhandle."

After her mom passed away, Mead realized she had to do something different, to make some kind of change. "I understand unhappy people," she says. "But I don't understand unhappy people who are scared of change." She didn't want to be unhappy 20 years down the proverbial road—not when there was an actual road leading somewhere else. "You only get one shot at this," she said. So she moved to San Luis Obispo.

Taking a $25,000 pay cut, Mead accepted a position as a winemaker at Talley Vineyards, south of SLO. In Santa Cruz, she'd been a production manager at a vineyard that produced 400,000 cases of wine. "That was never the type of winemaking that I wanted to pursue," she said. Talley Vineyards produces a tenth as many bottles a year. Today her responsibilities include overseeing everything that happens to the grape, from vine to bottle: the cultivating of the soil, the pressing and fermentation, the racking in French oak barrels. She tastes the product at several different steps along the way. She works closely with both fieldworkers and cellar workers to make sure each harvest is maximized for flavor. And then, because she's so familiar with the product, she becomes the face of the wine itself: Acting as sort of the head chef to Brian Talley's restaurant owner, she promotes the wine at tastings, market conventions, and restaurants.

A good winemaker, she said, is part farmer, part chemist, part craftsman, and part party host. It's an amazing job, so amazing that oftentimes it doesn't seem like work to Mead. "I can't think of another industry where people spend more of their personal time getting together to work," she said. "So many wine people are going to meetings to learn about the newest techniques at tasting groups, or how to improve your customer's palate—and nobody is getting paid for it."

As the Gallup poll suggests, happy people feel a sense of purpose on the job. The built-in social atmosphere of the wine industry has helped Mead forge a deep connection with her co-workers at Talley. And, like she says, much of it is voluntary: She started teaching an English as a second language program at Talley's farm, where she helps a few of the 250 farm workers with their skills. She's also a big part of the company's Mano Tinta (Red Hand) program, which directs proceeds from a special batch of red wine blends to the Fund for Vineyard and Farm Workers, an organization that helps worker families with housing, health care, and children's services. She also gives a lot of her time to a couple of "geeky wine groups"—the World of Pinot Noir and the Central Coast Wine Technical Group, where she swaps wine-production tips with her peers. "I feel really lucky that Talley gives me the type of latitude that they do," Mead says. "They believe volunteering is a positive thing for the company. If I were to work for somebody else and say I was going to be gone 10 or 20 hours a week during a critical time, I'm not sure they would let me do that."

Although she's happy at work, the other end of her commute is still important to her happiness. Mead lives with her husband and two dogs in a 120-year-old, two-bedroom house on the edge of a 40-acre vegetable farm (happy people are married, but don't necessarily have children). The couple exercises together by taking long walks around the beautiful big farm, but they avoid getting dirty. "We can look at how the cabbage is coming in, see the broccoli coming in," she said, "but we don't have to do the work." Happy people often have hobbies (which helps them stay connected socially), but while Mead's husband flies remote-controlled sailplanes (airplanes without motors) competitively, she says that she doesn't have a hobby of her own. And then she remembers that she does: Her hobby is wine, the ultimate social lubricant.

CITY WITH A MISSION

It's fitting that SLO's identity was built around an actual mission. The whitewashed walls of Mission San Luis Obispo de Tolosa rise from the hill in the center of the city. When it was built in 1772, this consecrated outpost was only one-fifth of what would eventually become 22 Catholic missions on the Camino Real. The Old Mission, as it's known to SLO-politans, is now the home church to more than 2,000 families and serves as the engine beneath the hood of a powerful tourism industry (tourism is the third largest employer in SLO County, behind government and agriculture). The Old Mission's pastor is Russell Brown, a 58-year-old former Dominican monk. Brown was raised as a Methodist and was working as a counselor for the University of California at Santa Cruz before deciding to change his personal mission.

San Luis Obispo: A Real American Dream

"Those ten years at the university went by so quickly," Brown said, "that I thought another ten or twenty could go by just like that." He joined the Dominicans, the same monastic order as that of Saint Thomas Aquinas, an order that has long been responsible for carrying the intellectual weight of the church. Aquinas was the Italian theologian who in the latter part of the 13th century first reconciled Aristotle's conception of happiness through virtue in this world, *eudaimonia*, with Christianity's belief that happiness is only possible through (and after) death. Aristotle further argued that happiness is something that you achieve, not something that you are. Aquinas was the first important Christian thinker to acknowledge that human happiness, albeit imperfect, could be actively attained through good works on Earth, a foretaste of salvation.

Brown believes there are a couple different routes to this earthly happiness. "You make a choice in life," he said. "You either do what you want to do and go wherever that takes you in the world, or you say, 'I want to live here, and I'll do whatever it takes to live here.'" Brown chose to change careers in order to further his life's mission in a new and meaningful way, which brought him to the actual mission in San Luis Obispo.

For many others living in San Luis Obispo, their mission is just that—to live in San Luis Obispo. On their first day of classes, Cal Poly students are warned, you're going to love it here, but after four years, you're probably going to have to leave. That's because of the limited economic opportunities in a town of this size and the competition created by people willing to make substantial sacrifices in order to live here, either by deferring home ownership for years or by participating in informal markets like "labor pools." I met one interior designer, for example, who traded her design work for dental work. Dan Krieger told me he had a hot tub put in, and the handyman he hired traded some computer work for the use of a cement mixer. The desire to live here by any means necessary may spur a special brand of creative entrepreneurship: SLO has far more self-employed people per capita than the average community in the United States. Bottom line, there is something more than long-term prudence implied in that foreboding first-day message given to the freshmen at Cal Poly: The underlying message seems to be that it's a special privilege to live in SLO. The people who live here believe that, and as a result, they seem to be really committed to living here.

Which brings us back to the fight over the central plaza.

A SEA CHANGE
By law, business signs in San Luis Obispo must be small and unobtrusive. In 1977, when Kenneth Schwartz was mayor, a new ordinance limited blinking lights and required that signage adhered to size restrictions. "Signs just beget more signs," said Pierre Rademaker, owner of Pierre Rademaker Design. And that's coming from the guy who designed the original Gap sign. I met Rademaker in his downtown office just before noon on a Friday, just as he was about to shut it

down, as he does every Friday at midday. Wearing blue jeans and a Hawaiian shirt, he somehow looked pre-relaxed when he told me, "I give everybody Friday afternoons off so we can run errands that would normally eat up your Saturday."

Rademaker decided to move to SLO 25 years ago, after getting stuck one too many times in bumper-to-bumper traffic on the Santa Ana Freeway in Orange County to the south. "I was 26, newly married, and living in a nice apartment," he said, "but we felt the need to go somewhere." And when he made it to San Luis Obispo he knew immediately: "I thought, 'I'm never going back!'"

A long daily commute tugs at the sweater of society, Rademaker believed. The longer the commute, the more rapid the unraveling. "You don't feel as connected to a city," he said. "When you get home from a half-hour commute to work, there's no way you're going to feel like going to a city council meeting." (Rademaker's intuition is right on: Psychologist Daniel Kahneman of Princeton found that on a daily basis, commuting ranks as people's *least* favorite activity, behind housework and child care. "Intimate relations" scored highest, followed closely by socializing after work and dinner.) But in SLO, there really wasn't a commute longer than ten minutes (and even if there was, as Shelly Stanwyck in the city manager's office told me, it was likely to be "gesture free.")

"Virtually everybody I know here is happy," Rademaker said, "and I think it may be because it's so easy to feel connected." He speculated that one reason was that people feel safe: "There's less fear than in other places—you don't worry about your kids going downtown." But more important, he said, people in SLO feel that they can actually make a difference. "It's easy to be involved," Rademaker said. "To feel like you have a voice."

Rademaker traced this feeling of empowerment back to Kenneth Schwartz. "It was that mission plaza that changed everything," he said. "Businesspeople opposed it hugely, but it turned out to be a bonanza for them." They didn't know they needed it, Rademaker said. "They wanted to stick to their agenda of keeping all the parking spaces and the highway, but the mission is our biggest draw: It attracts tourism. It created the space we use for concerts in the plaza. Every Friday during the summer there's a free concert with hundreds of people. Afterwards, the restaurants fill up." Rademaker credited Schwartz for giving the people something that Walt Disney was reviving in California around the same time: the central square. "In the fifties and sixties, we were tearing down main streets and town squares—exchanging these central public spaces for this anonymous sprawl. But Disney had awakened in us a sense of what we were tearing down. It became important to have a center again, a town square." But the most important thing the mission plaza changed was the way people thought about their own city. "If you look at our business community, it went from staid to progressive," Rademaker said. "But even better: After the referendum to close that street, people felt empowered to make change themselves."

A STUDENT PROJECT
THAT CHANGED A CITY

A wake-up call rarely makes anybody happy—certainly not at first—and it was no different for the people of San Luis Obispo. When I asked Schwartz if he could remember the moment the wake-up call happened, he leaned forward and said, "I can tell you precisely."

Schwartz remembered the day that three Cal Poly architecture students made a presentation to the city council in 1968. "As much as possible, we wanted our students to take on place-based, real-world problems," he said. The genesis of the plaza idea was a homework assignment almost 20 years earlier, when in 1949 Margaret Maxwell, a junior college art teacher, asked her students to look at the downtown and propose ideas where art could be used to beautify the city. "I think Margaret had in mind murals, fountains, that sort of thing," Schwartz said. A pair of Maxwell's students turned in a schematic, which showed Monterey Street in front of the mission closed and replaced by a public park filled with art and landscaping—a space they called Mission Gardens. By 1968, this idea had gained momentum, and sides were being drawn for and against, with most of the public, including Schwartz, in favor of closing the street and creating what was now being called Mission Plaza. However, most of the downtown merchants and the council majority favored keeping the street open. In fact, by 1967 the council had declined to reappoint Schwartz to the planning committee because of his position. "I suppose

I had grown more and more central to the controversy," Schwartz said.

Despite the heated nature of the debate, three architecture students decided to make the Mission Plaza their senior project. Schwartz was encouraging. "I felt that the idea of a plaza downtown would be an interesting, dynamic problem for the students to deal with," he said. "These students came across an organization called America the Beautiful, which provided small grants of money to stimulate students to promote their ideas on community beautification. They were awarded $500 on the condition that they get a matching $500 from a local community group," Schwartz said. "You know, needs for paper, pencils, gasoline, that type of thing. So they went to the city council, and the council which had been embedded in this continuous argument said okay, we'll give you 500 bucks, but on one condition: if you come up with multiple schemes, and one scheme has to show the street left open."

The students came up with several different ideas for a mission plaza. One of the proposals left the street open as requested. And the city council agreed to let the students make their presentation at a special study session open to the public. "So they have their big hearing," Schwartz remembered. "The council chambers are packed. This had become such a controversial item that it was filled with curious people, and there stood the students wearing coats and ties, trembling in their shoes," he said. "The mayor opens the meeting—all five of the council people are present—and the students put up their first proposal, their favorite. This proposal showed the street to be closed. The mayor is visibly agitated. His face was getting more and more red, and after three or four minutes into the students' presentation he gaveled the meeting to a halt, turned to the students, and said, 'You haven't done what we asked you to do. We want our money back!'" Schwartz paused to ask one of his professorial leading questions: "Can you imagine the effect that would have on the audience?" I shook my head again. "Well, they were dumbfounded: a mayor talking to a 21-year-old college student who was doing his best to make a professional presentation? And having this mayor stop the meeting and demand his money back?" Schwartz continued. "By sheer luck, one of the men in the audience was a former city attorney. He was a member of the mission's parish, and he was there because he'd heard so much about this plaza and he wondered how it would affect the ceremonies of the church—weddings and funerals. His name was George Andre, and he came from an old-line San Luis Obispo ranching family. George stood up, turned to the students, and said, 'They can't do that, and if

Happy Cities

Helping it be one of the happiest cities in the United States, Boulder, Colorado, has official policies that require the preservation of open space for parks and recreational activities as well as a renowned network of bikeways that are usable year-round.

they persist, I will represent you at no cost.' Now the mayor really just came apart. He didn't know what to make of this. He had been frustrated going in, and he gaveled the meeting to a close and walked out, leaving the other four council people just agape. And the audience was shocked—they came to hear a presentation, and to have it closed down without the benefit of being able to hear it! The obvious turmoil got them thinking in new ways."

The local newspaper picked up this story of the sensational town meeting, and rode it hard for weeks. A referendum committee of five, including George Andre and Schwartz, collected enough signatures to have the issue placed on the ballot for a vote by citizens. When given one more chance, the council majority refused to change its mind about closing the street in front of the mission, the referendum went to a vote of the people, and passed by a vote of nearly two to one. Monterey Street was summarily closed. The downtown business community was in a state of shock, and in 1969 Schwartz was elected mayor of San Luis Obispo. You didn't need to suck on a finger to know which way the wind was blowing now.

PUSHING LEADERS

When it came to the creation of the mission plaza, the process was as powerful as the result. The citizens of San Luis Obispo ended up being more satisfied with their city government than any other city in the Gallup Healthways index, and the reason probably had to do with the active role they took in their city. But the legacy of the mission plaza struggle was not only that council meetings became well attended, with a portion of each meeting devoted to public comment like the one in 1968. It was also that city government became more transparent and approachable, and SLO's citizens became galvanized for constant progress. Since the mission plaza referendum, they have consistently pushed their representatives to push for two key indicators of happiness according to the Gallup data: public health and access to outdoor recreation and the arts. In fact, people from SLO take pride in being national leaders in these areas.

In 1990, San Luis Obispo became the first municipality *in the world* to pass a smoking ban in workplaces, including bars. A council member introduced the law, but a private citizen introduced the idea. "I was at an American Medical Association delegates meeting," recalled Steve Hansen, the soft-spoken local doctor who was instrumental in the original 1990 ordinance as well as two more recent ordinances banning smoking on sidewalks and in parks, and soon after in outdoor public spaces generally. "And there was a presentation on the EPA report categorizing second-hand smoke as a group A carcinogen—putting it right there with benzene and asbestos and estimating that it would kill 50,000 Americans that year," he said. One of his former patients, a council member named Jerry Reiss, was already planning on introducing a more restrictive smoking section ordinance. "But I reminded him that, due to physical laws, smoke circulates like urine in a pool," Hansen said. "I urged him that if you're for public health, let's do the right thing that makes the most scientific sense. He agreed, and we got the total ban passed." Since then, smoking rates have dropped to 13.4 percent in SLO, fifth lowest of any town in the country.

A few years later, another citizen pushed for a ban on drive-through fast-food restaurants, and now the closest In-N-Out Burger joint is found in Santa Maria, 20 minutes down the freeway. San Luis Obispo has also been a leader in clean air legislation. In an attempt to lure smog-weary tourists (and, serendipitously, to make fast-food less convenient) from the Los Angeles basin, their city motto in the 1990s was "Come Up for Air." They continue to take their air seriously today, with tough restrictions on emission levels within all-new construction projects. Health-conscious, outdoors-loving SLO-politans have also demanded more biking and hiking trails, and to ensure that the sea-foam green hills those trails pass through just outside of town remain sea-foam green, they put in place a strict one percent growth limit that discourages megadevelopers from targeting SLO. The city has also negotiated with existing real estate holders to maintain a "greenbelt" around the city. Since 1994, the city has acquired 3,000 acres of open space. San Luis Obispo citizens ranked fifth slimmest in a recent poll, with an obesity rate of 17.6 percent, compared to the national average of 26.5 percent.

A city the size of San Luis Obispo "has no business having its own orchestra," said Barry VanderKelen, executive director of the San Luis Obispo County Community Foundation. "But it does." Access to the arts is a key contributor to well-being, the experts say, and maybe because it's right between Los Angeles and San Francisco, unclaimed by either cultural epicenter, SLO has to provide access to the arts on its own, without relying on a bigger municipality. In 1986, the city, Cal Poly, and the foundation for the Performing Arts Center came together to build an elegant, 1,289-seat concert hall on the edge of the Cal Poly campus. The venue has hosted a vibrant slate of classical music, opera, and pop. Around the corner from the mission, on the edge of mission plaza, sits the San Luis Obispo Art Museum, with two large galleries showcasing local and international artists, as well as space for rock concerts, art classes, and film seminars. Behind the art center, there's a small amphitheater receding into the hill

Happy Tasks

According to psychologist Daniel Kahneman's "day reconstruction method" studies (see "Gathering Joy" on p. 150), this is how people ranked a number of average daily activities from the most enjoyable to the least: socializing after work, relaxing, dinner, lunch, watching TV, socializing at work, talking on the phone at home, cooking, child care, housework, working, commuting from work, commuting to work.

over the creek where the Music in the Plaza summer concert series is held.

"A lot of our residents are newcomers," explains VanderKelen. "And they really fall in love with the place, and want to make sure that they stay in love with the place, so they invest in it."

Even the larger employers in SLO seem enlightened. On my last day in town, I made my way to Level Studios, an interactive digital agency with about 200 employees, with clients such as Apple, Cisco, Disney, HP, and BlackBerry. Doug Carr, Level's business development director, showed me around the building and told me about some of the perks that come with being a Level employee. Level has an innovative ride-sharing program and heavily subsidizes employee bus passes in order to take advantage of a well-run (and not too SLO) public transportation system, for example. Carr has a 17-minute commute himself, but it's not like a 17-minute commute in Los Angeles or San Francisco: "I have three decisions—do I want to see the oceans, vineyard, or mountains?" he said. The company also sponsors blood drives and 5K races and Beer Fridays, where the CFO brings in quality microbrews to sample and everybody can hang out and chop it up in the company kitchen a little bit (hanging out with your coworkers also ranks highly on Daniel Kahneman's enjoyment scale). But the thing that stuck with me about the company was when Carr told me that only five percent of his employees are actually born and raised here. "People choose to live here," he said.

San Luis Obispo: A Real American Dream

Leo Tolstoy famously begins *Anna Karenina* by positing, "Happy families are all alike; every unhappy family is unhappy in its own way." By deduction, this seems to imply that there's some sort of golden rule, some sort of *plan* all those happy families follow. But as Kenneth Schwartz points out, being happy in America is a funny thing: We value freedom to pursue happiness over any sort of planned happiness, even if the latter is a better guarantee of actual happiness. Our founding documents promise us that the pursuit of happiness is an inalienable right, but there's no plan to actually achieve it. Maybe our happy cities are like Russian happy families and they're all alike, but it seems that Americans feel a need to figure out happiness for themselves. It's that old tension between continental planning and Anglo-Saxon freedom.

As John Stuart Mill, the British philosopher who gave us *On Liberty* and who valued autonomy over any coerced felicity, once wrote, "Let any man call to mind what he himself felt on emerging from boyhood—from the tutelage and control of even loved and affectionate elders—and entering upon the responsibilities of manhood. Was it not like the physical effect of taking off a heavy weight, or releasing him from obstructive, even if not otherwise painful bonds? Did he not feel twice as much alive, twice as much human being, as before?" Mill understood that we can still listen to great teachers and look to great examples, but ultimately the most meaningful lessons are learned on our own.

The people of San Luis Obispo have already figured that out.

Lessons from San Luis Obispo

San Luis Obispo offers a clear example of how an American community can proactively change itself to create an environment where people live longer, happier lives. A student group galvanized citizens to push through a project that created a cultural and social focus for this city and, in so doing, improved the quality of its government. With more citizen participation, the town's focus shifted away from optimizing the business environment to maximizing quality of life. As a result, San Luis Obispo gained a more aesthetically pleasing downtown, with less traffic, less pollution, more gathering places, protected green spaces, a farmer's market, thriving arts, and an environment where it's harder to do things that are bad for you (smoke, eat fast food) and easier to do things that are good for you (walk, eat vegetables, recreate in nature, and bike). The result is arguably the healthiest and happiest city in America

A Civic Project Can Galvanize a Population

The mission plaza controversy and subsequent referendum ultimately brought the residents of San Luis Obispo together and taught everybody a lesson about citizen empowerment. One small project that rallies a community to make a difference can send a lasting message that citizens can have a voice in government.

Antismoking Policies Can Make People Happier

As the Gallup data shows, it's hard to be happy without your health. San Luis Obispo was the first city to enact antismoking legislation in bars. Other effective policies include strict citywide bans—no smoking in the workplace, in parks, and in front of office buildings. The idea was to "de-normalize" smoking, so if you're a smoker, no matter where you go, you're reminded that it's the wrong thing to do. This is consistent with findings that, although quit-smoking programs often fail at first, their success ratio climbs with repeated attempts. So workplace or city policies that support smoke-cessation programs will contribute to lower smoking rates in the long run.

Minimize Signs

As both Pierre Rademaker and Ken Schwartz argued, signs beget more signs. As one sign gets bigger, blinkier, and more distracting, the neighboring business is forced to make its sign even bigger and blinkier. With small, tasteful signs, SLO has not only made the city more aesthetically pleasing, but also ratcheted down the ubiquitous marketing, thus lessening the temptation to buy—a fleeting source of happiness. Research also shows that policies that limit fast-food signs decrease consumption of junk food, hence bettering people's diets.

Prohibit Drive-through Restaurants

A ban on drive-through restaurants has been on the books in San Luis Obispo since the 1980s. It was originally written to temper car culture in a college town, but the silver lining has been its effect on health, especially obesity and the myriad health care costs associated with the obesity epidemic. One of the easiest ways to lower obesity rates is to make the healthy choice the easiest choice. Making it impossible to drive up to a window to easily indulge a hunger pang with a cheeseburger also helps.

Build a Greenbelt

San Luis Obispo has an aggressive greenbelt plan in place, as well as an ordinance limiting housing growth to one percent a year. With help from the Land Conservancy of San Luis Obispo County, a city natural resources manager proactively raises money to buy close-to-town green spaces. This helps to eliminate the kind of suburban sprawl that plagues too many cities.

One of the biggest casualties of sprawl is recreation. A gym just can't replace convenient access to parks, hiking trails, mountain-biking trails, and wildlife preserves—beautiful areas both to enjoy and to get the body moving. SLO does a great job making all those areas so easy to see it's a constant invitation.

Support the Arts

Ken Schwartz is fond of quoting the Persian proverb, "If you have but two coins, use one for bread to feed the body and the other for hyacinths to feed the soul." Schwartz isn't just talking about growing flowers; he is talking about cultivating all kinds of art. Happy people have access to art—painting, film, sculpture, orchestra, opera, and rock and roll—and live in homes and communities that are themselves attractive to the eye. And in order to provide access, you need to build venues, or upgrade galleries, plant trees, or volunteer time. Around the world, there's a strong connection between populations that consume art and their level of well-being.

Favor the Pedestrian

Research shows that if you make the active option the easy option—good sidewalks, bike lanes, less and slower traffic—activity levels go up. In SLO activity levels are high because the mission plaza project closed the old Highway 101, because there are wide sidewalks, because there are bike lanes and cyclist rights-of-way, because new buildings require bike lockers and showers, because the bus stations are convenient, and because the bus pass system gives people who work downtown a free pass.

Make It Easy to Work for Yourself

Nearly a quarter of San Luis Obispo workers are self-employed (thus cutting down on commuting times). The more autonomy you have and control you have over your job, the more likely you'll be satisfied with your work. So start your own business and make your own plans.

Build a Town Square

At the same time that America's cities were spreading out into the suburbs, Walt Disney designed Disneyland's entrance to re-create the Main Street and town square of days gone by. In the same way, the people of San Luis Obispo refocused their town's resources inward to a mission plaza to give people a place to meet socially, to provide a venue for the arts, and to serve as an icon of civic pride.

CHAPTER SIX

Lessons in Thriving

Lessons in Thriving

We've heard from the top experts on happiness, met some of the world's happiest individuals, and explored places around the world where populations are verifiably thriving. Now what does this all mean to you? What lessons can you take away from this book to increase your own happiness? What can you learn from these stories to help you thrive?

As we discovered during our travels, recipes for well-being can vary dramatically from one culture to the next. In Denmark, citizens feel well cared for by their government, knowing their needs will be met for health care, education, and many other social benefits. More than that, Danes trust their public officials, just as they trust their neighbors, with whom they share a sense of equality about social status. As part of a wealthy society, Danes are able to slow down and enjoy the finer things, such as music and art, which contributes to their overall satisfaction with life.

By contrast, Mexicans don't have much confidence at all in their government, sharing a healthy distrust of the police, in particular, whom they view as corrupt or incompetent, especially in the face of today's rampant crime. Yet they still manage to experience high levels of well-being. To compensate for the shortcomings of their government, they rely on strong relationships with friends and family, on a supercharged faith in their church, and a remarkable capacity to laugh in the face of hardship. Even though their nation isn't as wealthy as many others, Mexicans still find the bright side of daily experience, which helps to lift them above all but a few nations in happiness ratings.

For people in Singapore, meanwhile, security and rapid economic growth have been the key to their good fortune. Determined to live up to their own high expectations, the citizens of this small island nation during the past 40 years have engineered one of the fastest growing economies in the world. The happiest people in Asia, they have accepted a broad range of restrictions on their personal freedoms in return for stability and safety. For them, happiness and success have become tightly intertwined.

The residents of San Luis Obispo, finally, have handcrafted a California lifestyle during the past few decades that actively promotes thriving. Deliberately aiming for the right balance between prosperity and the pursuit of happiness, the people of this relatively small college town have developed a taste for civic involvement, self-employment, fresh foods, local wines, and volunteering for good causes, with almost one in four residents donating their time to nonprofits. The result has been a boost in civic pride that has raised their level of well-being to one of the highest in the United States.

Despite their many differences, these four hot spots of happiness have each given us important clues about ways to improve our own well-being. Each has shown us what actually works in life's mix of ups and downs, and in the rest of this chapter we'll take a closer look at these strategies we can apply in our own lives. But before we do so, we must first come to grips with two powerful forces that can push each of us away from authentic happiness.

This first is our brain's hardwiring. Research has shown that when it comes to recalling happiness, our memories are unreliable: We tend to remember the high points and the low points of any experience, but not the minutiae in between. We tend to underremember everyday pleasures such as hanging out with friends or engaging in challenging work—what psychologists call intrinsic goods—while over-remembering fleeting pleasures such as the thrill of an award or buying something bright and shiny—what experts call extrinsic goods. When we look back on our Florida vacation, for example, we're more likely to remember the rude waitress at lunch and the amazing pool party than all of the relaxing hours we spent on the beach. That's why most of us spend too much time and energy going after a bigger house, a faster car, the latest fashion, a pay raise, or the newest electronic gadget—things that don't bring us lasting happiness.

The second force that subtly keeps us from thriving is the distracting nature of contemporary life. Each day the average American is bombarded by some 250 marketing messages encouraging us to eat things that aren't good for us and to buy things we don't need. Advertisements sell us an idealized vision of youth while vastly underplaying the wisdom that comes with age (as well as the greater degree of happiness, which peaks after retirement). Online social networks and the ever-increasing amount of time we spend watching TV have conspired to keep us in front of flickering screens instead of interacting face to face with other people. Elementary schools focus on teaching job skills rather than the arts, civics, and physical education—activities known to produce lifelong satisfaction. Perhaps the most compelling statistic to come out of recent happiness research is the fact that, during the past 35 years, while Americans have worked to increase our income by 20 percent, and the size of our houses has more than doubled since 1950, we've become no happier as a nation.

As worldwide research shows, individuals who thrive tend to possess enough money to cover their basic needs, but rather than striving for more cash, they focus their time and energy on developing a caring group of healthy friends, working at meaningful jobs, engaging in enriching hobbies, staying in reasonable shape, volunteering, and belonging to faith-based communities. Sounds simple, doesn't it? But reading about such things isn't enough: How do you make such nourishing activities a routine part of your life?

The answer lies in changing your *environment*. As you'll see in what follows, I'm going to suggest a number of ways that you can permanently set up your life to favor happiness—so that even after you forget about this book, the strategies that you put in place will still be working for you. After all, the world's happiest people don't take motivational courses to change their ways, nor do they rely on their genes to promote happiness. But they do live in environments—geographic, social, cultural, and physical—that constantly nudge them into pursuing intrinsic goods and other behaviors that favor long-term well-being.

So how can you set up your life so you'll spend your time on the right things and not chase empty promises of fleeting happiness?

To begin with, let's think about the different domains we live in. What are the main environments that influence what we do? In my research for this book, I've found six life domains that we can shape to boost our chances for happiness for the long term. I call them *Thrive Centers,* and they're all interconnected:

1. **Community**—The nation, state, county, city, or suburb in which you live. Does your government create an environment that helps you to feel good about your life and to live out your values?

2. **Workplace**—Your job site, or wherever you spend most of your working hours. Have you selected an engaging job that lets you exercise your talents without consuming you? Does your workplace environment facilitate meaningful work?

3. **Social life**—The circle of friends, acquaintances, and others with whom you come in contact regularly. Do your friends influence you to eat right, to be active, to laugh, and otherwise to reach your potential? Or do they load you down with negative feelings?

4. **Financial life**—The savings and spending strategies you adopt. Do you have too much easy credit or spending cash? Is it easier for you to save or to spend?

5. **Home**—Your house, apartment, or condo and the yard or grounds around it. Is your home set up to nudge you into behaviors that favor happiness and away from behaviors that generate discontent?

6. **Self**—Your education, sense of purpose, and health strategies. When it comes to happiness, does your inner self include a capacity for gratitude, openness to give and receive love, and an appreciation of the arts?

As we saw in Denmark, Mexico, Singapore, and San Luis Obispo, the world's happiest places tend to set up such Thrive

*The best way to promote Thriving is to set up "nudges"
favoring long-term happiness in all six domains of our lives,
Community, Workplace, Social Life, Financial Life,
Home, and Self.* ILLUSTRATION BY BLUE ZONES LLC

Centers so that individuals are constantly nudged in the right direction. In the pages that follow, you'll find a set of similar nudges to stack the deck in favor of your own happiness. Setting up these nudges will take some time and effort. But they will be well worth it as they guide you in subtle but powerful ways to greater well-being.

1. COMMUNITY

Traditionally, economists have measured the health of a nation by its gross national product. As conventional wisdom goes, the higher a country's GNP, the better off its people will be. And indeed, while people in wealthier communities are generally happier than people in poorer ones, the benefits of higher income for individuals tend to taper off once income rises above the level necessary to provide necessities. So if income's not the magic bullet, what is?

Where you live.

More than any other factor, including income, education level, and religion, the place where you live determines your level of happiness. As one study suggested, for example, if you're an unhappy person in Moldova—still reeling from Soviet repression decades ago—you're more likely to get a boost by moving to Denmark than you would be by staying put and winning the lottery, marrying the person of your dreams, or earning a Ph.D.

Results from surveys in 146 countries representing most of the world's population show that the top factors promoting happiness where you live are the following:

- **Economic freedom**—The freedom for citizens to start and run a business, free of excessive regulation, can be even more important than political freedom in determining happiness.

- **High employment rate**—Programs that give people jobs endow them with a sense of purpose and productivity. Unemployed individuals, especially the newly unemployed, suffer markedly lower levels of well-being. Singapore's "top up" policy has been shown to be effective at achieving higher employment rates. Conversely, places with generous social security systems are no happier than those with little or no social security.

- **Tolerance**—As we saw in Denmark, a nation in which citizens of all walks of life—religious, cultural, and sexual preference—are accepted is more likely to nurture happiness than one that allows discrimination.

- **Quality of government**—Fair legal institutions, a lack of corruption, trustworthy legal systems, and a strong democratic process all promote higher levels of happiness in a nation.

As a practical matter, most of us don't have the luxury or inclination to relocate to a different country. But many of us will move within our country. The average 18-year-old American, for example, will move nine more times in his or her lifetime, thus offering many opportunities to select a better environment.

If we're in a position to help our current communities thrive, on the other hand, there are specific things we can do to promote authentic happiness arising from personal growth, family relationships, and community interaction. The following are a few suggestions from economist Bruno Frey.

Provide More Community Space

As we saw in San Luis Obispo, a community that develops parks, vibrant city centers, outdoor restaurants, public gardens, and pedestrian malls makes it easier for citizens to socialize. Since we know that people are generally happier the more they socialize, the key is to make socializing the easy option.

Limit Shopping Hours

Purchasing new things brings only fleeting, extrinsic satisfaction. By limiting shopping options, we can free up time and resources for intrinsic pursuits. Frey suggests limiting how long stores may stay open. Denmark and the Netherlands, two of the world's happiest countries, set the maximum shop opening hours at 155 and 96 hours a week respectively.

Limit the Workweek

When it comes to long-term happiness, personal income fails to provide much of a boost for Americans once a household rises above the $60,000-a-year threshold. Individuals who work long hours have less time for social interaction, education, culture, sports, and volunteer work. They're also more likely to suffer chronic diseases and a poor family life. The Danish-mandated maximum of 37 hours a week is a good benchmark.

Support the Arts
A German study has shown a direct correlation between funding in the arts and the well-being of private citizens. Art gardens, theaters, dance centers, museums, and even street artists not only provide venues for social interaction, but also cultivate authentic happiness.

Encourage Walkability
Any policy that nudges people to live closer to their workplaces increases life satisfaction. Healthy people are happier people. Research shows that cities that build sidewalks, add bike lanes, and create a feeling of safety—making the active option the easy option—tend to increase the activity levels of residents. A few ways to do that: tax fuel, provide tax incentives for living near workplaces, and limit investments in augmenting traffic.

Grant Maternity Leave
Laws that mandate maternity leave not only help to foster stronger family relationships, but also help to assure that newborns get a good start in life. Research has shown that early interaction between parents and children is critical to a child's development. Mexican law provides 12 weeks of paid maternity leave. Danish law gives 18 weeks of paid leave to the mother and 2 weeks of paid leave to the father, with an option to take another 32 weeks of paid leave between them. In the United States, the Family and Medical Leave Act grants 12 weeks of leave, but it doesn't have to be paid leave.

Educate Teens About Birth Control

Out-of-wedlock births have long-term negative impacts on the financial and general well-being of parents. What's more, disadvantaged children are less likely to get a good education and more likely to commit a crime. Programs that teach birth control, distribute contraceptives, and provide reasonable access to abortions have been shown to reduce teenage out-of-wedlock births.

Drilling down to the neighborhood level, the location of your home can strongly influence your daily activities and, hence, your well-being. Here are some characteristics of a good neighborhood:

- **Sidewalks**—Look for sidewalks and bike lanes that connect homes. You're more likely to keep physically fit. (Activity levels in walkable communities are as much as 35 percent higher than in communities where it's hard to get around.) It's also easier to be social—you don't have to cut across the lawn or walk into traffic to interact with your neighbor.

- **Quiet surroundings**—Move to a quiet neighborhood. Humans are supremely adaptable creatures. We can get used to an ugly street or subfreezing weather (Minnesotans are happier than Floridians). But humans don't adapt to noise. In other words, jet planes overhead, buzzing transmission lines, honking traffic, or loud music from next door promise a daily erosion of happiness.

- **Walking distance**—Again, if it's easy to access intrinsic goods, you'll consume more of them. Go to the website www.walkscore.com, type in your address, and see how walkable your neighborhood is in terms of the distances to churches, parks, grocery stores, and museums.

- **Safety**—As we saw in Singapore, a sense of safety was critical for people's well-being. You might also look for a neighborhood where you'll feel comfortable letting your kids play outside. Also, research shows that the biggest deterrent to physical activity for some people is perceived danger. In other words, you want the outside environment to draw you out, not nudge you in.

- **Status equality**—Live in a neighborhood with your own economic class of people. As Denmark taught us, you don't want to be reminded of what you don't have. One study showed that people would rather make $50,000 a year and live among people who make $50,000 a year than make $100,000 a year and live among people who make $250,000 a year. If every time you drive down the street you see neighbors with nicer cars and bigger houses, you're more likely to want them, too.

2. WORKPLACE

Many of us spend more than half our waking hours at work, so finding the right job is one of the most important things we can do to influence our happiness. Data from the

Gallup-Healthways Well-Being Index, along with the analysis of some 1.3 million health claims, show that people who thrive have 20 percent lower health care costs. Moreover, the happiest people at work are also the happiest people at home. Here are a few ideas for getting the right job and the most satisfaction from that job.

The Right Job
In tough economic times like these, any job may feel like a good one. But as we've seen in Denmark, Mexico, and San Luis Obispo, other factors besides a paycheck determine how much satisfaction we get from our jobs in the long term. According to Claremont University psychologist Mihály Csíkszentmihályi, finding a job that challenges us to an optimal level—one that's neither so hard that we give up nor so easy that we get bored, that engages our natural talents, and that gives us constant feedback—is a sure way to build happiness. You're more likely to enjoy a job over the years if it addresses your passions, values, and talents rather than simply giving you a big paycheck, office, or title. Also, make sure you're working with the right people. The biggest predictor of whether or not you're satisfied with your job is whether you're working with colleagues with whom you can be friendly. Before you consider your next job, begin by answering the following questions:

- How is this work important?
- What can I contribute?
- What excites me?

- How can this work challenge me in an ongoing way?
- Would I do this work even if I didn't get paid?
- How does this address my passions?
- Would I think about my work even when I'm not working?
- Does this work make me feel proud?
- Can I achieve excellence at this?
- Can I forge a true friendship with the other people who work here?

The Right Way to Work

Here are some ground rules to make sure your job contributes to your overall happiness:

- **Avoid long commutes.** Commuting is the least favorite activity people do on a daily basis. In fact, people who commute an hour each way would need an additional 40 percent of their monthly wage to be as satisfied with their life as people who walk to the office. Try to find a job in your neighborhood or within an easy, fast commute, and you will set yourself up for minimal angst.

- **Limit your workweek to 40 hours.** Choose a job that's not going to infringe on family and social time or exclude other interests and hobbies. On the whole, part-time workers report more life satisfaction than full-time workers.

- **Don't skip vacations.** Vacations lower stress levels, rejuvenate us, and give us time to pursue a wider variety of interests. A

Danish study shows that we get the most satisfaction from an average of six weeks of vacation per year. The average American worker takes between 8 and 16 days of vacation per year! Research also shows that much of the happiness bump from vacation comes from the planning and anticipation. So if you have four weeks of vacation, you might increase your overall satisfaction by planning four weeklong trips instead of one big one.

- **Enjoy happy hour.** Socializing after work is one of the most satisfying activities we do on a daily basis. Try to find a workplace where post-work socializing with co-workers is the norm. Questions to ask during an interview: Do you like the other employees? Are there any employer-sponsored after-work activities? Do people knock off at five o'clock, or do they work incessantly?

- **Seek out the right boss.** A Gallup-Healthways poll showed that having the right boss is the single biggest determinant of workplace satisfaction. The qualities you should seek in a boss include the following:

  - **Approachability**—Can you talk to your boss about your challenges and problems?
  - **Provides regular feedback**—Does she tell you when you're doing a good job and offer constructive suggestions when you're not? Does she meet with you regularly?
  - **Establishes clear requirements**—Are your duties and

responsibilities clear? Do you know when you've suc-
cessfully completed a task?

- **Delegates control**—Does your boss get out of the way
  to let you do your job in a way that works for you?
- **Practices good listening**—Does he really listen to your
  ideas? Is there open communication?
- **Offers recognition**—Are good work, productivity,
  and innovation recognized?
- **Earns your trust**—Do you trust your boss?
- **Considers your best interest**—Does your boss care
  about you as a person?

Employ Yourself

Self-employed workers and business owners report some of the
highest levels of well-being. It may be because they have control over their own work and are more likely to pursue work
that they love, or simply because they are their own best bosses.

Get into Teaching

Teachers score higher on most aspects of well-being than
people in nonteaching jobs such as sales, manufacturing,
farming, and so on—even higher than self-employed business
owners. They view their lives more positively, express more
optimism, and report a healthier life. This may be because
they derive great satisfaction from a school's social environment and from helping prepare the next generation for life.
Or it might be simply because the teaching profession attracts
happier people.

3. SOCIAL LIFE

One of the most dependable, universal means to a thriving life is simply to socialize more. Data from Gallup-Healthways polls on well-being show that the happiest Americans socialize six or seven hours a day—especially with family and friends. An analysis by Nicholas Christakis, a social scientist at Harvard, and James Fowler, a political scientist at the University of California at San Diego, showed that in a network of more than 12,000 people living in a small Massachusetts town, the happiest people were also the most connected. As their social circle got happier, so did they. (Conversely, in another study, college students randomly assigned to a mildly depressed roommate became increasingly depressed over a three-month period.) Even introverts tend to be happier when they are around people than when they're alone, studies have shown. So for the vast majority of us, setting up our lives to make it easier to socialize will augment the joy in our lives.

The quantity of social interaction is only half the prescription. Quality matters, too. Who we hang out with has an enormous and measurable influence not only on how happy we are, but also on how fat we are, or even how lonely we are. On any given Tuesday night, we can sit in a bar and listen to an old acquaintance's problems, or we can spend that evening going to the theater with an upbeat friend. According to one statistical analysis, each additional happy friend we have in our social circle boosts our cheeriness by nine percent, while each additional unhappy friend drags it down by seven percent. As we saw in Denmark, having trustworthy friends is critical. And as we saw in Mexico, surrounding ourselves with friends that have a sense of humor can also soothe stress and hardship. (Laughter has been shown to produce an insulin-like growth factor chemical—one that acts as an antidepressant and anxiety reducer in rats.) Recent research has also shown that we're likely to get more satisfaction from friends with whom we can have a deep conversation. Such conversations, experts speculate, may help more to make sense of our chaotic world and connect meaningfully with people than ones in which we gossip about celebrity scandals. Since friends are long-term adventures, surrounding ourselves with the right people, and engineering our lives so we spend more time with those people, should have a profound, long-term impact on our happiness.

In fact, just being around happy people is going to impact our well-being. Behaviors, it seems, spread partly through subconscious social signals that we pick up from those around us. For example, we tend to automatically mimic what we see in the faces of people surrounding us—which is why looking at a photograph of smiling people can itself often lift your mood. So, just hanging out in a café with upbeat people can improve your mood.

Here are some strategies to create the right kind of social bonds.

Upgrade Your Social Network

Consider making a list of the ten people with whom you spend the most time. Then, knowing that certain moods and behaviors are contagious, rate each friend on how lonely, depressed, trustworthy, or funny he or she is, and how likely you are to have a deep conversation with each. Now rank that list in order of the most positive to the most negative. That will give you a good idea about whom you should spend your time with. If you can't think of a friend with positive attributes, then it's time to widen your social circle. I wouldn't tell you to dump your old friends, but I can tell you that if you cultivate your relationships with the people at the top of the list, you're more likely to become a thriver.

Join a Club
Identify your interests or talents and find an organization that will nurture them. Make a commitment to a club or organization that compels you to show up regularly—through either the organization's rules or peer pressure. According to one study, joining a group that meets even once a month produces the same happiness gain as doubling your income.

Create Your Own *Moai*
Create a group of mutually committed friends—what the Okinawans call a *moai*. Okinawans, among the world's longest-lived people, travel through life together in clusters of a few friends. They commit to meeting regularly, share spoils in the case of a windfall, and support each other in times of crisis or grief. As part of an experiment in well-being, the town of Albert Lea, a community of 18,000 in southern Minnesota, created some 70 *moais*. Each group shared interests (some were new mothers, or liked to volunteer, or liked sports). Then

they made a point to walk together several times weekly for ten weeks, so that bonds could form in their groups. A year later, more than half the Albert Lea *moais* are still together.

Reconnect with Your Faith

Just about every study done on the connection between religion and well-being shows that the two go hand in hand. While we're not sure if churchgoing makes you happy or if happy people tend to be religious, research shows that people who belong to a faith-based community—regardless of the particular faith—and attend at least four times per month may live as much as 14 years longer than people who don't. Churchgoers are less likely to engage in risky behaviors (which can lead to profound unhappiness), are satisfied with less money, have less stress, and—to the point of this section—have built-in social networks. You'll amplify benefits if you join the church choir, volunteer as a greeter, or commit to read for the congregation. If you don't belong to a church or have drifted away from the church of your birth, seek out a new church that matches your current values and worldview. Start by asking friends or people you admire to make some suggestions, and try a new church in each of the next eight weeks.

Marry the Right Person

For most of us, choosing the right mate is one of the biggest reasons for our happiness. People in a long-term, committed relationship suffer less stress. A survey conducted in 2004 showed that 42 percent of married couples described themselves as "very happy," compared with 17 percent of divorced people and 23 percent of people who never married. Researchers Hyoun K. Kim of the Oregon Social Learning Center in Eugene and Patrick C. McKenry of Ohio State University found that national survey data showed that marriage helps protect psychological well-being. In other words, making the effort to find the right mate and to commit for life favors happiness. This is not to say that marriage assures bliss. Marry the wrong person, and happiness levels plummet, along with long-term health. (Bad marriages have been shown to increase stress, which in turn increases the risk of cancer and heart disease.) How to find the right person?

- **Kiss lots of frogs.** Ruut Veenhoven hypothesizes that people in urban areas enjoy a greater opportunity to date a wide variety of people before they choose their mate. The point here is to date a lot of people who you think align with your values and interests.

- **Look more than skin deep.** We're genetically wired to be attracted to certain characteristics that favor short-term sexual attractiveness rather than long-term bliss. While his big muscles and her pretty face may sing virtues on the surface, a sense of humor and compassion are more likely to keep you in the relationship for the long run.

- **Marry someone similar to you.** A recent study in the *European Economic Review* showed that people who have similar tastes and earning abilities, and who share things equally, have a better chance at marriage survival. This may suggest that if you like folk dancing, try to find a mate who also likes folk dancing—or marathon running or late-night TV. Look for partners who make as much money as you do, or at least are inclined to share what they have. If you're already married, working with your partner to find common interests should stack the deck in your favor. Also, partners who regularly attend church together are more likely to stay together. So, if you're a churchgoer, seek another churchgoer. A family that plays and prays together stays together.

- **Avoid cohabitation.** While leasing before buying may work for car purchases, the same is not true in shopping for a mate. A study that looked at a large number of successful and unsuccessful marriages found that living with a prospective spouse seems to make for a shorter, lower-quality marriage.

- **Try marriage training.** Learning early in the relationship how to deal with conflict and listen effectively ("If I understand you correctly, you just said . . . ") will stack the deck in favor of a successful marriage. A study of American marriage training programs found that only 4 percent of couples receiving the instruction had split up after five years, compared with 25 percent of partners that did not have the training.

- **Nice reminder.** Saying something positive to your spouse keeps a marriage vital.

Be realistic about the joys of parenthood
Next to our spouse, our children are the people with whom
we spend the most time. Contrary to conventional wisdom,
having children does not automatically bring us greater happiness. In fact, it can often be the reverse. Research shows that
during the first year of a child's life both the mother and the
father experience an increase in life satisfaction, but that soon
changes, and a reduction in general happiness occurs for both
parents—presumably from the added financial, relationship,
and responsibility stress—and mothers tend to be less happy
than fathers. In fact, women find caring for children less pleasurable than jogging and only slightly more pleasurable than
doing the dishes. The good news for parents is that happiness
seems to rebound when children turn 18. The rewards of par-
enting, it seems, are not easily measured on a happiness scale.

4. FINANCIAL LIFE
Summing up all the available research on the connection
between money and happiness, Ed Diener says that the key
to greater well-being is to *have* money but not to want it *too
much*. So the best long-term strategy for financial affairs puts
in place the disciplines and mechanism that help you save
mindlessly and spend thoughtfully. Here are some ideas.

Pay Off Your House
The average American household has nearly $70,000 in
mortgage debt. Although financial planners may argue that

your mortgage payments are tax deductible, and therefore your house can be a ready source of credit to underwrite purchases and better-returning investments, making a monthly mortgage payment can also be a regular source of anxiety and stress. When it comes to experienced happiness, it's more important to manage daily stress than to build up net worth. People who pay off their mortgages go to bed at night knowing that in the event of a catastrophe they will always have a roof overhead. Moreover, in today's economy, there's no assurance that even a savings account will outperform the five percent or so that we currently pay on our mortgages.

Enroll in Automatic Savings or Investment Plans
Make sure you're subscribed to your employer's retirement plan if one is offered. If you're not, consider a plan that automatically deducts from your paycheck (credit unions and most banks have such plans). If you can save just sixteen dollars a week beginning at age 18 and invest it in an S&P 500 Index fund, you will retire a millionaire at age 65 (given historical rates of return).

Avoid Credit Cards
The average American household has a debt balance of more than $8,000 on a whopping eight credit and debit cards! You should have one credit card, and it should not be in your wallet. Put it somewhere that requires a conscious effort to retrieve it (for example, your locked glove compartment or a hidden pocket in your purse). When you pay cash for a purchase,

actually counting out those bills, you *feel* the purchase. You're less likely to spend frivolously on a new shirt you don't need or a just-released gadget. Moreover, if you pay cash you'll be less likely to go into debt—a sure source of ongoing stress.

Create a Giving Account

In their book *Nudge,* economist Richard Thaler and former law professor Cass R. Sunstein propose the creation of a "giving account." The idea is to deposit a sum of money—say $1,000—at the beginning of the year. We mentally commit that money to our favorite charity, to be donated at year's end. But if, in the intervening 52 weeks, we get a parking ticket or traffic violation, or have other sorts of annoying "life is unfair!" mishaps, we can pay for them out of this giving account. Since we know that mitigating day-to-day stresses will increase experienced happiness, and since research shows that we get more satisfaction from spending on others than spending on ourselves, this annual discipline will stack the deck in favor of greater long-term happiness.

Invest in Experiences

Spending your money on family vacations, dance classes, ongoing education, music lessons, scuba diving, and so forth is more likely to provide you with a lasting sense of well-being than buying the latest fashions or splurging on a new car.

5. HOME

What if you could set up your home in a way that would enhance your well-being just by your living in it? Once again, the trick is knowing the often counterintuitive habits that research shows lead to happiness and then organizing your home to propel you gently toward those behaviors. Here are some examples.

Fewer TV Screens

Have only one TV in your house. Ideally it would be located in an out-of-the-way room in a cabinet. Take the TVs out of your kids' rooms. Research shows that this will likely reduce your child's body fat index by nudging them into being more active. Remove the TV from the kitchen, too. This reduces mindless eating and excessive calorie consumption.

Cancel Cable

An Israeli study suggests that when TV viewers are confronted by the paradox of too many choices on cable TV, they are more satisfied sticking with basic TV. As TV watching increases, so do worries about children and a sense of guilt.

Own a Pet

Many studies suggest that pet owners are healthier and happier than people without pets. Pet owners have been shown to have lower blood pressure and fewer stress hormones in their blood. In fact, the presence of a pet was found to be more effective than a spouse or a friend in easing the effects of stress on the heart. Pets foster self-esteem, calmness, soothing, and a feeling of acceptance. They provide daily, nonjudgmental companionship and a means for us to take the focus off our own needs and problems. Pet-owning seniors suffer fewer minor health problems, need to see the doctor less often, and enjoy lower health care costs. If a dog needs to get walked every day, guess who else tends to get walked?

Create a Meditation Space
Regular meditation has been shown to activate areas of the brain that register pleasure and to inhibit parts of the brain that register pain. There are several forms of meditation, some as simple as mindfully counting your breaths or slowly scanning your body head to toe and acknowledging each body part. Establishing a dimly lit, quiet space where you can sit comfortably will make daily meditation more accessible.

Designate a "Flow" Room
As we learned earlier, Mihály Csíkszentmihály describes the experience he calls "flow" as a state of engagement in which you're using your talents, optimally challenged, consummately interested, and able to let time melt away. I recommend you create a room that will promote such flow. Taking a cue from family rooms in Denmark, you could establish a room where it's easy to play an instrument, to take part in a hobby, to read a book, or to play a game with family. Place a large table in the middle of the room to accommodate the whole family's projects. Line the room with books. Lose the clock, TV, computer, or any other gadget that takes your mind off engaging activities. Make it the most aesthetically appealing room in the house (with the best light and the nicest furniture) so you'll naturally be drawn to spend time in it.

Lessons in Thriving

Create a Pride Shrine
Set up one area of your house to routinely remind you of the people, accomplishments, and events of which you are proud. In my home, I've created a shrine of sorts, inspired by Okinawan ancestor shrines. I first identified the private part of my house that gets the most traffic (the hallway between our bedrooms and bathroom). Then I built a display table and designated wall space. There I display pictures of my kids, my beloved grandmother, my college diploma, my daughter's report card, a ribbon I won for greased-pig wrestling in ninth grade. You get the idea. Every time I walk by, I'm rewarded with a surge of pride and a reminder that I'm part of a family continuum.

Grow a Garden
Several studies show that gardening lowers stress hormones. Hoeing, planting, weeding, fertilizing, and harvesting all occasion regular, low-intensity, range-of-motion exercise. It's one of those nudges that encourages almost daily activity for at least four months of the year. And you end up with healthful vegetables!

Let the Sunshine In
Maximize sunlight by creating outdoor areas (patio, lawn chairs) for basking and big, south-facing windows for indoor sunlight. Emerging research shows that sunlight prompts manufacture of endorphins that give you a feeling similar to a runner's high. It also promotes the manufacture of vitamin D—a compound most Americans lack in sufficient quantities. Just a few minutes

of quality sunlight on the face and arms (only between May and September in northern latitudes) provides more vitamin D than a gallon of milk. And while it's difficult to get enough quality sunlight through the window for vitamin D production, window-filtered sunlight hitting the retina will still help raise spirits and mitigate against seasonal affective disorder.

Paint Your Mood

A great deal of research has been done on color and mood. Painting your living room yellow will inspire energy and a bright mood. Paint areas for meditation and rest a soothing color to promote relaxation. Japanese hospitals are painted a healing shade of sea-foam green.

Optimize Your Bedroom for Sleep

The average person should sleep six to seven hours per night for optimal health and well-being. Your bedroom should be primarily for sleeping. Free it from TVs, computers, brightly glowing clocks, and other distractions. Make sure it can get dark and cool. If reading helps you sleep, keep books and magazines nearby. Also, make sure the light is within arm's reach so that if you begin to nod off, you can switch off the light without getting up and spoiling your slumber. Finally, minimize use of the alarm clock. You'll feel best if you let your body wake you up.

6. SELF

The goal here is to train yourself in a few areas that will yield well-being benefits for the long run. Take time to recognize your values, strengths, talents, passions, and gifts. Your personal sense of purpose may be something as simple as seeing that your children or grandchildren grow up well. It could also come from a job or a hobby, especially if they are challenging and satisfying. If you set out to learn a musical instrument or new language, you get a double bonus, as both have been shown to help keep your brain sharper longer. "Exercising your brain is important," explains neuropsychologist Paul Nussbaum of the University of Pittsburgh. "You should especially find things to do that are novel and complex. Once you get good at them, and they are no longer novel, then you can move on to something else. So you're kind of doing strength training for the brain, which has been shown to decrease your rate of memory loss and maybe even decrease the rate at which one might develop Alzheimer's Disease."

Here are some ways to create a thriver's mind-set.

Personal Mission Statement

Start by articulating your personal mission statement. First, answer this question in a single, memorable sentence: What is your reason for getting up in the morning? Richard Leider, the best-selling author of *The Power of Purpose,* recommends that you take a personal inventory by using this formula: G + P + V = C. His research suggests that in order to know your core sense of purpose, you first need to have a clear understanding of your core values—your Gifts (what you have to offer the world), Passion, and Values equals your Calling. "Are you using your GIFTS on something you feel PASSIONATE about in an environment that VALUES you? If so," Leider says, "you're *on purpose*. You have a reason to get up in the morning!"

Find a Purpose Partner

Find someone to whom you can communicate your life purpose as well as a plan for realizing it. "Think of one person who has the capacity to give you that periodic wake-up nudge to the potential of your life," Leider recommends. "Make a practice to talk with the 'Purpose Partner' about your life purpose two or three times a year."

Develop Arts Appreciation

Learning to appreciate the painting of favorite artists can set you up for a boost in happiness every time you see their works. Taking time to listen to your favorite composers can do the same. Even learning the history and rules of a sport (stats, superlatives, backgrounds of the players) can give you a richer and long-lived appreciation than that of the casual sports fan.

Find a Hobby

We should all have a hobby that enhances our work life. As we saw in Denmark, 95 percent of Danes belong to a club, many of which are organized around common interests such as model trains, jumping rabbits, or playing chess. Some Danes even knock off work at mid-afternoon to spend the rest of the day engaged in a hobby. This offers life another dimension that wholly caters to our interests and talents. It helps us get into the state of flow and increases both evaluated and experienced happiness.

Develop Your People Skills

Learning people skills such as how to build consensus, how to listen constructively, and how to feel compassion for others sets you up with tools to build and maintain a social circle. Dale Carnegie's *How to Win Friends and Influence People*, for all of its salesman overtones, offers several pieces of genuinely good advice—like remembering people's birthdays with a card, calling people by their first names, and asking people about themselves.

Volunteer

One of the surest ways to increase your well-being is to volunteer. It can boost your happiness. Volunteers tend to weigh less, to feel healthier, to have less chance of suffering a heart attack, and to score higher in every happiness domain. Volunteering takes the focus off of your own problems and increases your sense of pride in your community or social network. If you're not a volunteer now, start small. Volunteer once a month at your church or local social service. As you feel the benefits, research shows, your involvement will likely grow of its own accord.

THRIVING CHILDREN

Armed with such insights from the emerging science of happiness, we can now think about ways of raising our children to favor long-term happiness. American schools currently emphasize math, science, and language arts. No one disputes the importance of these skills, but how about skills that we know more directly yield well-being? How can we help our children identify and begin to pursue their own sources of flow? How much TV and computer time should we allow them? And later, how can we help them think about a job that's right for them? What qualities should they look for in a mate?

So far, such research has been scant. But here are a few of the evidence-based clues that have emerged to help us raise happier kids.

Put Friends First

A recent study published by the Gallup organization showed that student well-being has little or no relationship to income. Over half of what explains well-being in children is how engaged they are socially. So, as this study suggests, helping our children find and maintain good friendships is one of the most powerful things we can do for them. Moving into a safe neighborhood with lots of kids the same age will better enable kids to make friends on their own. Establishing friendships with parents of the children who we'd like to see play with our children is also a good long-term strategy.

After-school or Summer Job

When your children become teenagers, encourage them to find a job that interests them. Babysitting, lawn mowing, bagging groceries, or working at a local café are all jobs open to teens. Such experiences teach teens an appreciation for money, help to build self-confidence, instill independence, and expand a young person's social circle. A Boston study that followed inner-city kids for more than 20 years found that the only common denominator among the happiest people was having had a high school job. Education level, profession, income, and marital status were not as strong as happiness predictors.

Music Lessons

Nudging kids into the musical arts at an early age can not only give them a bump in academic performance, but also set them up for a lifetime of enjoyment.

Civics and Arts Appreciation

Since we know that engagement in the arts and participation in government favor well-being as an adult, giving our children tools that facilitate these two disciplines prepares them for fulfilling adulthoods.

Instill Hope for a Richer Future

Shane Lopez, a Gallup senior scientist, has found a clear connection between hopefulness and financial literacy. Kids who see a bright, meaningful future start to earn, keep, and save money better than those who don't. Such kids come up with more ideas about how to make money, become more pragmatic when using money, and are more creative in saving money. How can parents help?

- by getting their kids talking about what they want to do when they grow up
- by asking their children for ideas about how to realize their desired future and work through obstacles
- by showing genuine excitement about their children's dreams

Moms seem to do this better than dads, Lopez says.

Encourage Sports

Because of school busing on the one hand and funding cuts for gym classes on the other, we've engineered much of the physical activity out of our children's lives. That makes it increasingly important for parents to make sure children get involved with organized sports. A recent study showed that when teenage girls participate in sports, it helps them succeed later in life. Female athletes have higher rates of employment and higher education, and playing sports also reduces their risk of becoming obese.

NUDGING YOU TOWARD HAPPINESS

I started this book by introducing you to Panchita, the wood-chopping, machete-wielding, 103-year-old Costa Rican woman with the whooping laugh. I remember the first day I met her. It was a bright morning, and I walked to the edge of the town of Hojancha and onto a footpath that led to her jungle shack. I could smell roasting tortillas and hear the tinny, syrupy *sabanero* music from a transistor radio wafting out of nearby houses. On the footpath, a resident troop of howler monkeys languished in the mango trees overhead. When Panchita saw me, she pushed open a wooden shutter and, with her hands raised, exclaimed, "Oh, how God blesses me. A visitor from America!" And then she hurried out into the courtyard to hug me. "Come sit down," she said, and took a seat on the wood-plank bench outside her house. She was wearing a festive, frilly dress—green this time instead of pink. Long, green earrings dangled from her ears, and she had her gray-tinted hair pulled back with a rhinestone-studded comb. We spent several hours together. She told me about her life—the years working in a travelers' lodge, the murder of her son, and the time when, at age 76, she beat up a local drunk for watching her bathe. "I gave it to him good," she said with a pointed finger. Through-out the conversation, she called me Papi and, to make a point, endearingly put her hand lightly on my arm.

Later that morning, a woman stopped by to help her sweep her floors. "I don't come here because I have to," the woman told me. "Panchita has a way of making my day happier."

At noon, Panchita announced it was time to make lunch. I followed her into her simple, two-room house: a bedroom with a table and chairs, a bed with tattered sheets and blankets and pictures of Jesus on the wall, and a kitchen. The kitchen was simple and pleasant, with two windows that opened onto the yard. Panchita cooked on a wood-burning stove next to a wood counter, a soapstone sink with cold running water, a small pantry, and a modest refrigerator. She hand-ground corn, heated up beans, and fried the only two eggs she had. Then she presented them to me. "Eat!" she commanded. Before I dug in,

I realized that it was the only food in her kitchen, and I persuaded her to eat it.

I'd sought out Panchita because I'd been looking for clues to explain how she'd managed to arrive at her 11th decade with so much vitality. But now I realize that I'd overlooked something important. In addition to maintaining her excellent diet and active lifestyle, Panchita was also thriving—experiencing authentic, lifelong happiness—which, as I've learned since, can add about ten extra years to a person's life expectancy. And although some of her positive outlook might be due to favorable genes, I also realized that her surroundings deserved most of the credit. Growing up on the Nicoya Peninsula, she'd been born into a culture of faith where God gave her life a clear meaning. She'd earned enough money to cover her basic expenses, but certainly not enough to tempt her into any frivolous spending. Her home had been loaded with nudges that kept her moving all day—from the hand grinder for the corn to the stove fed with wood—and her neighbors had offered her daily social interaction. Her porch had provided her with many sunny afternoons. Panchita's environment, in short, had shaped her for happiness.

There's a lesson here for you: You can shape your own environments to live better longer, too. The best way to do that, as we've seen, is to follow the practices of the world's most experienced thrivers: Set reasonable goals for your life. Seek out a place to live where people are already thriving. Choose a community where you can live out your interests. Find a modest house in a neighborhood of other modest houses, with neighbors you can call friends and sidewalks that let you walk where you need to go. Recognize your purpose in living each day. Take time to appreciate the arts. Find a job that you love without worrying too much about the salary. Find a hobby that fuels your passions. Take six weeks of vacation no matter what. Set your life up so that you're physically active every day. Spend six hours a day with your lover, kids, and a handful of TRUE friends. Meditate, pray, or nap daily.

And call your mother.

Afterword

Even in the year since the first printing of this book our understanding of happiness has evolved remarkably. New places have emerged among the happiest in the world, including Costa Rica and Canada. We've discovered that, as we get older, our happiness follows a U-shaped curve: We start off happy in our early years, are least happy at middle age (45 seems to be the worst age on average worldwide), and then we grow happier again in our later years. New evidence has confirmed that the experiences we have—which tend to gain luster with time—bring us more happiness than the things we buy. But perhaps the most exciting finding of all concerns the very definition of happiness and how we experience it through two selves, the *remembering self* and the *experiencing self*.

Consider the remembering self—how we remember our lives. To identify the happiness hot spots I profile in this book, I relied largely on measurements of the way we experience this self. I worked with three worldwide databases that aggregate well-being surveys asking people to score (usually on a scale of 1-10) how satisfied they are with their lives. It's a valid measurement: Who better to assess our happiness than ourselves? The problem is that we remember our lives imperfectly. We tend to remember high points, low points, and the most recent things that happen to us. The smell of a new car and the feeling of driving it off the lot, for example, is etched more deeply in our memories than, say, the monthly payments for the car or the thousands of times we empty our wallets to fill the gas tank. Daniel Kahneman, the Nobel Prize-winning psychologist who has done some of the most innovative research on happiness, reckons that a typical psychological moment lasts about three seconds, which means that we can expect to have more than 500 million moments in the course of a 70-year life. There's no way to keep track of so many moments. (Quick: Can you remember what you had for lunch a week ago Tuesday?) In fact, Dr. Kahneman estimates that we remember only about 3 percent of our past. Which raises a good question: If we can't remember our lives accurately, how can we expect to set realistic goals for ourselves or make credible plans?

Hence the experiencing self.

The experiencing self is how we live our lives moment-to-moment, day-to-day. To measure this kind of happiness,

Dr. Kahneman and his colleagues outfitted subjects with an electronic device that prompted them at random moments to describe what they were doing and assign an emotion to it. He found that, on a day-to-day basis, what people most enjoy is sex (surprise, surprise!) and socializing after work. They least enjoy housework, child care, and commuting to work.

Another way to measure the experiencing self is to ask people to remember things they did yesterday (the assumption being that we can pretty accurately remember yesterday) and assign them positive or negative emotions. Interestingly, people who remember their lives happily don't actually always experience their lives happily and vice versa. Research provides a good example here: Millionaires as a whole will rate their remembering selves higher than people who make only $75,000 a year. But the millionaire may have a bigger house to look after, a heftier financial portfolio to look after, and a higher-maintenance spouse, so he or she may in fact experience life less happily.

This insight about the difference between the remembering self and the experiencing self sheds new light on both the happiness of nations and the happiness of individuals. Just a few weeks ago, I heard from Ed Diener, the preeminent psychologist from the University of Illinois at Urbana-Champaign. He'd looked at several recent years of happiness data for most of the world's nations. Denmark once again tops the list of the world's happiest places—but only in how Danes remember their lives. Costa Ricans experience more happiness in their lives than any one else on the planet. One might conclude that hardworking, trusting, socially minded people—like northern Europeans—tend to remember and evaluate their lives as being happy. Meanwhile warmer, more laid-back peoples—like Latin Americans—experience their lives with more happiness. Sierra Leone and the nation of Georgia have the worst of both worlds.

Remembering Self

Below are rankings for countries by life satisfaction. Subjects are asked to consider their life as a whole and to score it on a 1-10 scale.

Experiencing Self

Below are rankings for countries by *positive feelings*. Subjects are asked to remember how much enjoyment they felt yesterday, as measured by laughing, smiling, etc.

➕	➖	➕	➖
Denmark	Sierra Leone	Costa Rica	Georgia
Finland	Haiti	Canada	Armenia
Netherlands	Tanzania	Paraguay	Serbia
Canada	Zimbabwe	Laos	Sierra Leone
Sweden	Georgia	Ireland	Bosnia
New Zealand	Chad	El Salvador	Lebanon
Australia	Burkina Faso	New Zealand	Azerbaijan
United States	Mali	Argentina	Montenegro
		Venezuela	

To gain more insight into the difference between how we remember happiness and how we experience happiness, I teamed up with a rising star in the science of happiness, Ryan Howell, a statistician and psychologist from San Francisco State University, and Matt Bartel, a gifted programmer, to create the True Happiness Compass *(bluezones.*

com). First and foremost, the True Happiness Compass is an online tool to help identify how your lifestyle is affecting your well-being—by either increasing or reducing your life satisfaction, your ability to flourish, and your daily emotions. It asks you to answer approximately 70 short questions about your work and personal life, your home, and your interests. Then it gives you a score for both your remembered happiness and your experienced happiness. It also suggests personalized changes that you can incorporate into your daily routine to optimize your overall happiness.

So far, more than 14,000 people around the world have taken the Compass. By analyzing their answers—taking into consideration their age, gender, education, wealth, and the number of positive and negative life experiences—Dr. Howell was able to identify which characteristics accompany both experienced and remembered happiness. (If you were doing these things, in other words, you were telling us you're happy). The happiest people were able to:

- Explain their life purpose in one sentence.
- Have more than four close friends who are happy.
- Socialize at least six hours a day.
- Have daily sex.
- Spend some time every day in nature.
- Watch less than one hour of TV a day.

Using the same data, we also looked at a number of other characteristics that we believed might influence happiness. We found that while making more than $75,000 a year has an impact on your remembering self, it doesn't have an impact on your experiencing self. Meanwhile, how much time you spend on online social networks such as Facebook and whether you own a dog or a cat has a big influence on your experiencing self and no real influence on your remembering self. Overall, we found the happiest people:

Spend less than 30 minutes a day on screen time — The happiest people spend no more than half an hour a day watching TV or playing video games. After two hours of screen time a day, happiness really drops off. People who spend more than four hours are the least happy.

How much time in the average day do you spend watching TV or playing video games?

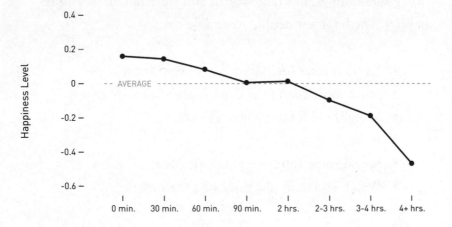

Afterword

Spend minimal time on online social networking — As in TV watching, the happiest people are those who spend only 30 to 60 minutes a day participating in online social networks such as Facebook. The least happy are those who spend three or more hours on online social networks and no time on face-to-face interactions.

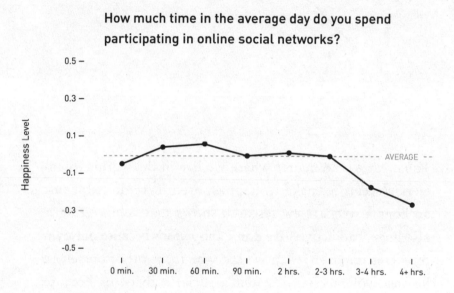

Listen to Music — The happiest people listen to music for at least two hours a day. It doesn't seem to matter if it's jazz, classical, rock, alternative, or Peruvian windpipes.

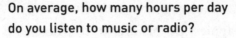

On average, how many hours per day do you listen to music or radio?

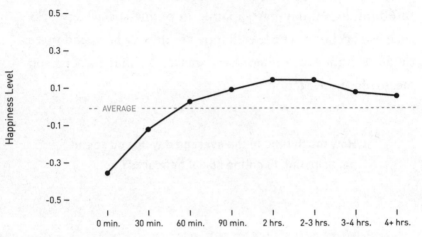

Volunteer — No matter where we live in the world, volunteering seems to make us happier, even if we do it for just an hour a week. (New research shows that volunteering is also hugely addictive.) We don't know if it's because our own problems diminish when we take the focus off of ourselves, because volunteering is often a social activity, or because there's just something inherently enjoyable about helping others. The message is clear: As little as two hours a week of volunteering is likely to make you significantly happier.

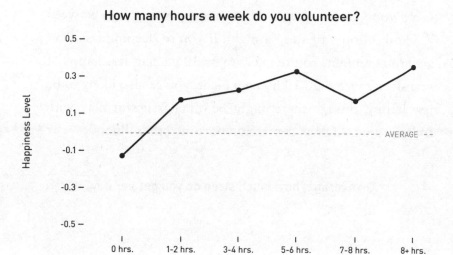

How many hours a week do you volunteer?

Have a diverse social circle — Having just one friend of a race or ethnicity different from us makes us measurably happier. Having at least three such friends makes us even happier. Viva diversity!

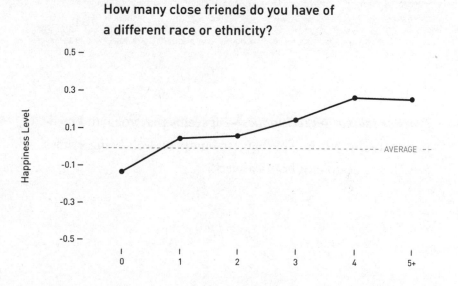

How many close friends do you have of a different race or ethnicity?

Get a good night's sleep —The average person needs between 7.5 and 9 hours of sleep a night. If you're sleeping less than six hours a night, you're likely to be 30 percent less happy. If you sleep more than 10 hours a night, you're also likely to be less happy, though there might be other issues at play with oversleeping, such as depression or some other illness.

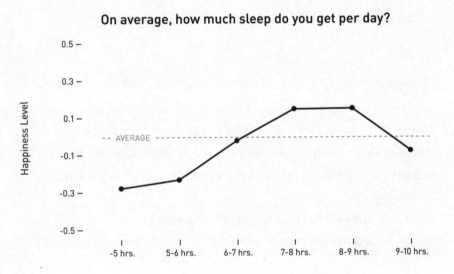

On average, how much sleep do you get per day?

Practice relaxation techniques — It seems that yoga and meditation really work. The biggest bump in well-being comes after just a couple of hours a week.

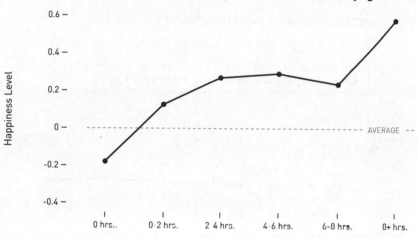

How many hours per week do you meditate or practice other relaxation techniques such as tai chi or yoga?

Take enough vacation — The biggest happiness surge comes from taking any vacation (rather than none at all). The happiest people overall take at least four weeks of vacation.

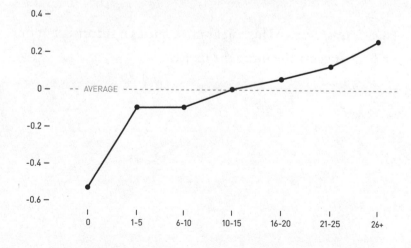

How many vacation days do you take per year?

Read books — Reading a book at least every other month helps to keep the blues away. Such people report being 9 percent happier than those who never read books.

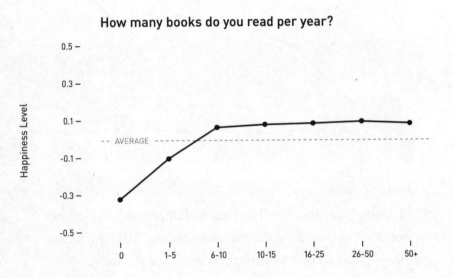

How many books do you read per year?

Have lots of sex — This might not come as a surprise, but our findings suggest the more the better.

How often do you engage in sexual activities?

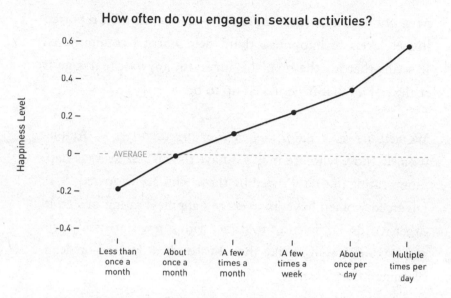

And on the topic of love, we've gotten *Men Are from Mars, Women Are from Venus* news from Mexico. Nicole Fuentes, who researches happiness in Mexico, sent us some preliminary results of a study on love and marriage. She interviewed some 500 people in the state of Colima, asking them about their attitudes on marriage and divorce while also rating their happiness on a scale of 1-10. Her study suggested that:

It's worst to be separated — Both men and women reported the lowest levels of happiness when they were undergoing a separation—the in-between stage between marriage and divorce.

Men are happiest when divorced — Divorced men reported higher levels of happiness than their married counterparts. It seems that for the men she surveyed, anyway, marriage is really not all that it's cracked up to be.

Women are least happy when they are divorced — Among women, those who are married have the highest average happiness rating (8.6), followed by those who are widowed (8.4). Divorced women have an average happiness rating of 7.9. In other words, Dr. Fuentes told me, with a few statistical caveats, "Women seem to like their husbands at home—or dead. Nothing in between."

Note to self.

Reading Group Guide

Author Dan Buettner sets out upon a plan of study that is both intriguing and illuminating. In his quest to *Finding Happiness the Blue Zones Way*, he seeks answers to the following questions:

- Which types of governments yield the greatest happiness dividends for citizens?
- Which cultural values foster the greatest degree of life satisfaction?
- What role does religion play?
- How about money?
- What's the optimal mix of communal tradition and individual choice?
- What can the world's happiest peoples tell us about what makes a difference in their lives? (page xiii)

Before you begin your travels through this Reader's Guide, lay out your own floor plan as to what will make for a happy life, a happy community. Start by answering the questions listed above for yourself. Be an active participant in the author's search for the secrets of happiness.

Thrive

Chapter One: The Truth About Happiness

1. Buettner reveals that "according to the Gallup organization, 'thriving' countries are those whose citizens think positively about their lives and report more happiness, enjoyment, interest, and respect" (8).

   On a scale of 1 to 10, with 10 being the most positive and 1 being the least, how do you rate your overall happiness level, the level of respect you receive in your community, and the level of interest you have in the world around you?

   Now, following the suggestion of Jim Harter, coauthor of *Wellbeing: The Five Essential Elements*, predict where these ratings will be in five years. Spend a few moments and contemplate what these answers say about you as an individual.

2. Sonja Lyubomirsky, author of *The How of Happiness: A Scientific Approach to Getting the Life You Want*, says that "the true keys to happiness lie in changing the way we think and behave, seeking out experiences such as savoring a beautiful moment and taking a picture of it, thanking a friend, writing a gratitude journal, or performing random acts of kindness" (14).

   When was the last time you thanked a friend for what he or she has done for you? When was the last time you performed a random act of kindness?

   Exercise: Over the next week, commit a daily random act of kindness (visit a nursing home, put change in a row of vending machines, drop off a toy or game at a local hospital); write a letter to a friend expressing your gratitude for what they've done for you.

Begin creating a "Gratitude Journal." Write in it each night before bed. What are you grateful for in the day just passed, what are you grateful for in the day to come? Make sure to include your reactions to your random acts of kindness as well as your letters of gratitude.

3. Mihaly Csikszentmihalyi, the director of the Quality of Life Research Center in Claremont, California, says that "true happiness involves the pursuit of worthy goals. Without dreams, without risks, only a trivial semblance of living can be achieved" (15).

What are your goals? What are your dreams? In the long term? In the short? Reflect upon this. Do these goals reflect a level of "true happiness" that you are satisfied with? What would you like to see change if anything?

Chapter Two: Denmark: The World's Happiness All-Stars

1. Peter Gundelach, a sociologist from the University of Copenhagen, says that "enlightenment came early" to Denmark (34). He believes "a lot of it goes back to the period after 1864, after we lost 25 percent of our territory to the Germans . . . We had to abandon our ambitions to be a superpower" (34).

How is abandoning ambitions to be a superpower tied to enlightenment? What are your ambitions? Are these curtailing your happiness?

2. His Royal Highness of Denmark, Prince Philippe de Bourbon-Parme has a son who "found his passion in woodwork" (47). When Buettner asks why he didn't push his son into doing something "more regal," the Prince responds, "Whatever for? I want him to be happy with what he does" (47).

   Do you push yourself toward more lucrative, respectful, or safe choices for your future? Do you push your own children likewise? Have you been pushed by your society, by your family to make such choices?

3. After dinner, Erik Kristiansen's family traditionally moves out to the backyard by a fire pit: "This is the time my family usually talks about their day. We're away from the food and confusion and the daily schedules. This is the time we connect" (61).

   What is your family ritual after dinner? How much time do you spend with the television? Your kids with video games? When do you sit back and just talk? How often do you connect?

   Exercise: Reserve a time each day for your family to sit down to connect. You don't have to have an elaborate tradition like the Kristiansen family. Sit down for ten, fifteen minutes at the outset. Write about this in your Gratitude Journal. Then watch as the tradition grows and develops on its own merit.

Reading Group Guide

Chapter Three: Singapore: Can You Manufacture a Happy Nation?

1. Singapore puts great emphasis on work as they pursue "the five C's: cash, credit card, car, condominium, and club membership" (78). Jennie Chua, the CEO of Raffles Holdings Ltd, a model of Singaporean success, says that "the five C's are just a more glamorous way to provide for our families . . . For so long, it was such a struggle to put a roof over our heads, food on the table, and get our kids educated . . . The new generation has evolved and become less transactional. They spend weekends with their kids and are beginning to see the value of volunteering their time" (93).

   Clearly, the people in Singapore worked extremely hard to establish a world for themselves where they can now spend time with the family. How much time do you spend away from your own family in order to build a world for them? When is the time when you've provided enough, when you can step back from your own "five C's" and cherish what you have built?

2. "The Malays have something called the Kampong Spirit," says Ahmad Nizam Abbas. "In the past, we used to live in fishing villages called kampongs, where we pulled together to help each other during times of adversity or disaster or during times of celebration, like preparing for a wedding. This notion still survives . . . If something happens to a Malay household, within a few hours the whole Malay community will be there to lend its support" (97).

   What is your village like in terms of community spirit? How much support do the people of your immediate area offer one another in times of adversity or celebration? Can you think of any way to foster a more community-minded spirit of kampong in your area?

3. Buettner sees a large difference in the makeup of Asians as opposed to Americans. "For Asians, striving for personal happiness appears to be a vaguely impolite and selfish concept that falls somewhere near the bottom of a list of lifetime goals. For Asians, the individual exists only in the context of his family and community. The individual is not separate. He is often driven toward perfection, but not for personal gain as much as to live up to societal expectations, and to make his mother proud" (114).

Exercise: Create a list of what you strive for in terms of achieving happiness. Afterward, take time to note how many of these items are personal, how many are geared toward society and how many are geared to family. What would you like to change over the next few years?

Chapter Four: Mexico: The Secret Sauce of Happiness

1. Buettner reveals that "a recent study carried out by Gallup-Healthways shows that social time massively affects day-to-day happiness. It suggests that for most people spending six to seven hours in social time each day helps to maximize their well-being" (137).

Compare your work schedule to your social schedule. How many hours do you put in at the office each day? How often do you get together with friends and neighbors? Are you as productive socially as you are at the office? What do you think your annual social review would be like? What would you like to change over the next five years in these respects?

2. Buettner visits with several women in a poor neighborhood who sit out on cinder blocks and chat in the afternoon. When he asked a young woman what she would do if she had a great deal of money, she first responds by saying she would buy a larger house; after a moment's reflection she decides against this because then "we probably wouldn't meet like this every afternoon" (151).

How important are the people of your community as compared to your home? How often do you see your own neighbors? How many shared challenges do you have? How much time do you put into the makeup of the house you live in as opposed to the relationships you have with your neighbors?

3. Buettner visits a young girl known as La Niña, who is renowned for creating miracles for her followers. "She addresses their pain and dispenses hope, the poor man's most valuable commodity. People leave feeling that they've been heard, that someone cared, if only for just a few minutes. For her followers—the poor and uninsured—La Niña provides a powerful dose of pain mitigation. And, as novelist Carlos Fuentes once said of his native country, it is impossible to understand Mexico without appreciating what it is to believe in miracles" (159).

How much do you believe in miracles? When was the last time you completely did? How was the world different? Would you like it to be so again?

Chapter Five: San Luis Obispo: A Real American Dream

1. Psychologist Daniel Kahneman of Princeton "found that on a daily basis, commuting ranks as people's *least* favorite activity, behind housework and child care. 'Intimate relations' scored highest, followed closely by socializing after work and dinner" (189). The list went as follows, from most enjoyable to least: socializing after work, relaxing, dinner, lunch, watching TV, socializing at work, talking on the phone at home, cooking, child care, housework, working, commuting from work, commuting to work.

   Where do you rate these areas on your own scale? Now, try to design an immediate future where you can begin to maximize your joys while minimizing the areas that bug you.

2. The people of San Luis Obispo created a mission plaza in the center of town which brought the community together. But it did more than that. As Pierre Rademaker, a local business owner, says, "After the referendum to close that street, people felt empowered to make change themselves" (190).

   What does it take for you to want to make a change in your own lifestyle? When was the last time you discovered this power? What about your lifestyle would you like to change?

3. The people of San Luis Obispo are very involved in the governance of their community. "With more citizen participation, the town's focus shifted away from optimizing the business environment to maximizing quality of life" (200).

Reading Group Guide

If you were empowered to make changes in your local community regarding green spaces, traffic, pollution, and the arts, what would you do? What is keeping you from doing it now?

Acknowledgments

My first thanks goes to Peter Miller, my editor at National Geographic. He promoted the idea for this book within the Society and then helped shape the prose. If not for him, this book would not have materialized. Similarly, without data, research, and encouragement from Dr. Ruut Veenhoven, curator of the World Database of Happiness, and from Dr. Ed Diener of the University of Illinois, and Dr. Ronald Inglehart, director of the World Values Survey, this project would have never gotten off the ground. I'd also like to thank the University of Zurich's Dr. Bruno Frey, Claremont Graduate University's Mihály Csíkszentmihályi, and Dr. Sonja Lyubomirsky of the University of California, Riverside, who all believed enough in the idea of this book to give me access to their research and countless hours of their time. Justin Smith, Nikki Duggan, Anne Wilkins, Janet Calhoun, and Ben Leedle all provided insightful interpretation of their Gallup-Healthways Well-Being Survey.

At National Geographic I especially want to thank Lisa Thomas who marshaled this book through its many stages, Nina Hoffman, who championed it at the highest levels, photo editor Susan Welshman, who knows why I'm thanking her, über publicist Laura Reynolds, and photographer David McLain, my close collaborator, who put his soul into this story. I am deeply grateful to Howard Schneider, who helped get this book off the ground, and to my researcher, Michelle Harris, whose dedication and insight protected the accuracy of my facts. Anders Weber, Jesús Lopez, Sonya Pedersen, and Sharon Lim set up dozens of interviews for me in the field, gained impossible access, and interpreted cultural nuances with relentless can-do pluck.

At Blue Zones the amazing Amy Tomczyk managed the book's endless logistics. Researchers Jennifer Havrish, Jessica Brehmer, and Amanda Jansen helped find and organize some 300 research articles. And thanks to business guru Tom Gegax, the best life I ever saved, and cameraman Emmanuel Tambakakis, the best life I almost failed to save.

In Denmark, Remar Sutton, my mentor and friend, permitted me into his rarefied circle of Danish friends, including Joseph de Palme, Silvia and Jock Munro, who have since become my friends. The Copenhagen Consensus's Bjørn Lomborg, Dr. Christian Bjørnskov, Dr. Jonathan Swartz, Martin Agerup, Jonathan Allen, Dr. Peter Gundelach, Dr. Rolf Jensen, Dr. Tim Knudson, Dr. Steen Navbjerg, and Dr. Uffe Østergård all gave of their time and knowledge.

Singapore's grand dame, Jenny Chua, opened many doors for me, both literally and figuratively. Douglas Foo shared not only his story but also the best sushi on the planet. Dr. Ho Kong Weng, Professor Kwok Kian Woon, Dr. Tan Ern Ser, and Singapore's lady of letters, Sylvia Lim, were all generous with their time. A special thanks goes to the infinitely gracious Celina Lin, who took me under her wing and guided me through Singapore's rarefied upper class. And thanks to Minister Lee Kuan Yew, who took a chance and granted me an interview.

Dr. Alejandro Moreno, Dr. Mariano Rojas, Enrique Serrano, Joaquina Palomar, Margarita, and Jesus Garza Arocha all helped illuminate Mexico's happiness. Mostly, I want to thank Nicole Fuentes

Acknowledgments

in Monterrey, who not only provided the best insights but also the best jokes.

A special thanks to Bill Weir and Rob Wallace at ABC's *20/20*, Morgan Zalkin and Patty Neger at *Good Morning America*, Leslie Grisanti with *Oprah*, *AARP* magazine's Nancy Graham, CNN's Sanjay Gupta, and my good friend Dr. Oz for thinking enough of my work to cover it.

The San Luis Obispo chapter wouldn't have come together without collaborator Steve Marsh. I'd also like to thank John and Dianne Conner for the Provence-inspired hospitality at their Petit Soleil hotel and Lindsey Miller at the San Luis Obispo Chamber of Commerce.

Finally, I thank Marty Davis; Tommy Heuer; Tom Moudry; John and Larisa Thurston; Mark McGuire; Nick, Steve, and Tony Buettner; Dr. Roland Engel; Dr. Jack Weatherford; Mary and Maureen Petricca; Gayle Winegar; Stephanie Pearson; Rob Perez; Rudy Maxa; Will Steger; Ed McCall; and especially Kelly Hegna, who supported me through the writing of this book and are my testament to the central tenet of this book: If you want to be happy, surround yourself with happy people.

Bibliography

Argyle, Michael. *The Psychology of Happiness*. Routledge Kegan and Paul, 1987.

Bok, Derek. *The Politics of Happiness: What Government Can Learn from the New Research on Well-Being*. Princeton University Press, 2010.

Buettner, Dan. *The Blue Zones*. National Geographic, 2008.

Christakis, Nicholas A. *Connected: The Surprising Power of Our Social Networks and How They Shape Our Lives*. Little, Brown and Company, 2009.

Diener, Ed, and Robert Biswas-Diener. *Happiness: Unlocking the Mysteries of Psychological Wealth*. Blackwell, 2008.

Kahneman, Daniel, Ed Diener, and Norbert Schwarz. *Well-Being: The Foundation of Hedonic Psychology*. Russell Sage Foundation, 1999.

Klein, Stefan. *The Science of Happiness: How Our Brains Make Us Happy—and What We Can Do to Get Happier*. Marlowe and Company, 2002.

Layard, Richard. *Happiness: Lessons from a New Science.* Penguin Press, 2005.

Leider, Richard J. *The Power of Purpose—Creating Meaning in Your Life and Work.* Berrett-Koehler, 1997.

Lyubomirsky, Sonja. *The How of Happiness: A Scientific Approach to Getting the Life You Want.* Penguin Press, 2007.

McMahon, Darrin M. *Happiness—A History.* Atlantic Monthly Press, 2006.

Myers, David G. *The Pursuit of Happiness—Discovering the Pathway to Fulfillment, Well-Being, and Enduring Personal Joy.* HarperCollins, 1992.

Nettle, Daniel. *Happiness: The Science Behind Your Smile.* Oxford University Press, 2005.

Schwartz, Barry. *The Paradox of Choice: Why More Is Less. How the Culture of Abundance Robs Us of Satisfaction.* New York: HarperCollins, 2004.

Thaler, Richard H., and Cass R. Sunstein. *Nudge: Improving Decisions About Health, Wealth, and Happiness.* Penguin Books, 2008.

Weiner, Eric. *The Geography of Bliss: One Grump's Search for the Happiest Places in the World.* Twelve, 2008.

Index

Illustrations are indicated by **boldface**.

A
Abbas, Ahmad Nizam 96–98, 116
Afghanistan 121
Aging *xii*
Alaska 51
Alaya, Adriana Pérez 154–159
Albania 18
Albert Lea, Minn. 226–227
Algeria 168
Alzheimer's disease 237
Ancestor shrines 235
Andersen, Hans Christian 51
Andre, George 193–194
Aquinas, Thomas 187
Århus, Denmark 3, 5, 51–53, 56, 58–60, 67
Aristotle 10, 187
Armenia 18

Art gardens 217
Artmann, Michael 56–57, 72
Arts
  access to 195, 196–197, 203
  appreciation 35, 49, 70–71, 122, 207–208, 212, 238, 241, 245
  support and funding 203, 217
Asia
  happiest countries 87
  see also Singapore
Aztecs 143, 153

B
Bangladesh 87
Basáñez, Miguel 134–138
Beder, Denmark 54
Bedrooms
  optimizing for sleep 236
Belarus 18
Bhutan 77

Bicycling 26–28, 36, 179–181, 204
Bike lanes 26, 148, 203, 204, 217, 218
Birth-control education 218
Biswas-Diener, Robert 79
Bjørnskov, Christian 53
Blackman, Marc 260
Blood pressure 155, 233
Blue Zones
  happiness 19–21
  longevity *x, xi*
Books and reading 13, 58, 234, 236
Boulder, Colo. 193
Bourbon-Parme, Joseph de 47
Bourbon-Parme, Philippe de 45, 47, 48
Brown, Russell 186–187
Buddhism 122
Buddhist monks 77, 169
Bulgaria 18

C
Cable TV 233
California. *see* Loma Linda; San Luis Obispo
Canada 31
Cancer 228
Cantril, Hadley 11
Carlsen, Jørgen 55–56
Carnegie, Dale 239
Carr, Doug 198
Castro, Mari 150
Centenarians *x, xi*
Chichimecas 161
Chihuahuan Desert, Mexico 129, 159
Children, thriving 239–242
China 82, 87, 105, 106, 107, 109, 112
Christakis, Nicholas 224
Christianity 168, 175, 187
Chua, Jenny 91–93, 116
Chumash people 175, 176
Churchgoing 147, 227, 229
Civic projects 200–201
Civil rights 67, 121
Climate, suicide rate and 132
Clocks 58, 234, 236
Club membership 36, 50, 71, 78, 226, 238
Coahuila (state), Mexico 129, 143
Cohabitation 229
Color, mood and 236
Community
    as life domain 211
    lessons in thriving 214–219
Commuting 17, 150, 189, 197, 221
Computers 234, 236, 240
Confucius 113

Conner, Dianne 179
Conner, John 179–180
Conrad, Joseph 92
Contentment, pursuit of 164, 171
Copenhagen, Denmark 25–28, 39, 44, 51, 61, 67, 71
Cortés, Hernán 143
Costa Rica *ix, x,* 31, 242
    see also Nicoya Peninsula
Credit cards 231–232
Csíkszentmihályi, Mihály 10, 15, 17, 55, 70, 220, 234
Cycling. *see* Bicycling

D
Day of the Dead 138
Democracy 22, 35, 36, 50, 132, 215
Denmark xiii, 3, 25–72, 207–208, 212, 214
    arts appreciation 70–71, 207–208
    club membership 36, 50, 71, 238
    family rooms 59, 234
    folk schools 35, 49–50, 54–55, 57, 59, 70–71
    hobbies 41, 58, 63, 64, 228
    job satisfaction 48, 63, 70, 220
    lessons from 66–72
    maternity leave 217
    shop opening hours 216
    social benefits 43, 68–69, 72, 207
    status equality 39, 68, 207, 219
    taxes 32, 33, 37, 42–43, 49, 70, 72

tolerance 38, 67, 215
trust 32, 43, 53–54, 67, 124, 207, 224–225
Díaz Ordaz, Gustavo 135
Diener, Ed 9, 11, 12, 15, 16, 18, 79, 153, 230
Dimitri, Prince (Russia) 45
Disney, Walt 190, 204
Dominicans 187
Donaldson, John 46–47
Dopamine 183
Drive-through restaurants 196, 202

E
Economic equality 68
Economic freedom 126, 136, 215
El Catón. *see* Fuentes Aguirre, Armando
El Niño. *see* Fidencio, José
Endorphins 165, 235
Espinazo, Mexico 154
Eurobarometer 22
European Values Study 21
Exercise 64, 235
Experienced happiness 169–170, 231, 232, 238

F
Faith therapy 168–169
Family, importance of
    Mexico 147, 162, 170–171, 208, 225
    Singapore 84, 87, 105, 120, 126
Fast foods 196, 200, 202

Index

Fidencio, José 153–154, 157

Financial life
as life domain 212
lessons in thriving 230–232

Finland 31

Flow, finding 55–58, 234, 238

"flow" rooms 234

Folk schools 35, 49–50, 54–55, 57, 59, 70–71

Foo, Douglas 116–119, 120

Fowler, James 224

Frederiksen, Claus Hjort 42–43

Freedom
happiness and 69, 142, 166
see also Economic freedom; Political freedom

Freedom of choice 142, 166

Frey, Bruno S. 10, 17, 216

Friends, time spent with 147, 150, 170, 171, 183, 212, 224–226

Fuentes, Carlos 159

Fuentes, Nicole 144–148, 167

Fuentes Aguirre, Armando 160–164, 171

G

Gade, Louise 52–53

Gallup-Healthways Well-Being Index 182, 194, 219–220

Gallup World Poll 22, 64

Gardening 235

Gardens, public 216

Gender equality xii

General Social Survey 168

Georgia, Republic of 18

"giving accounts" 232

God, belief in 147, 153, 168

"greenbelts" 196, 202–203

Gross national product 77, 145, 214

Grundtvig, Nikolai 34–35, 54, 55, 59, 70

Gundelach, Peter 29–31, 32–37, 40, 45

H

Haiti 134

Hammer, Jan 3–4, 5–6

Hansen, Steve 195–196

Happiness
Blue Zones 19–21
children and 186, 230
control over 13
definitions of 10–11
experienced happiness 169–170, 231, 232, 238
factors contributing to 14–15
freedom and 69, 142, 166
humor and 140–141, 166–167, 225, 228
measuring 11–12, 21–22, 80, 145, 150, 197
money and 16–17, 48, 133–134, 146–147, 167–168, 210, 230
polls and surveys 21–22

remembered happiness 169, 209
world's happiest places 31

Happy hour 170, 222

Harter, Jim 10, 11, 14

Healers, child 153–159

Hearst, William Randolph 180

Heart disease 228

Hemmingsen, Jørn Munk 61–66

Hiking trails 180–181, 196, 203

Ho Kong Weng 86

Hobbies 186, 210, 221, 234, 237, 238, 245

Hojancha, Costa Rica ix, x, 242

Holstein-Ledreborg, Marie 48–49

Home
as life domain 212
lessons in thriving 232–236

Home-based businesses 204

Home ownership 122, 188
see also Mortgage payments

Hong Kong 102–103, 112

Hormones 167, 233, 235

Hørup, Viggo 40

Human Development Index 133, 144

Humlebaek, Denmark 42–43

Humor, happiness and 140–141, 166–167, 225, 228

hygge 39, 54, 60

I

Iceland 31

Idalia, Silvia 150–151
Ikaría, Greece xi
Immune system 19
India 82, 106, 109, 112
Indonesia 87, 112, 124
Inglehart, Ronald 125, 130
Investment plans 231
Iraq 18
Islam 104
  see also Muslims
Italy 39
  see also Sardinia

J
Jante law 38–39
Japan 103, 109, 236
  see also Okinawa
Jensen, Rolf 37–39
Job satisfaction 14, 69–70, 204, 220–223
  Denmark 48, 63, 70, 220
  Mexico 137, 220
  San Luis Obispo 182, 184–185, 209, 220
Jordan 168
Junk food 4, 202
Jutland Peninsula, Denmark xiii, 50
  see also Århus

K
Kahneman, Daniel 150, 189, 197, 198
Kampong Spirit 96–97
Kim, Hyoun K. 228
Kipling, Rudyard 92
Krieger, Dan 180, 188
Kristiansen, Erik 59, 60, 61
Kristiansen, Esther 59

Kristiansen, Hannah 59, 60
Kristiansen, Peter 59, 61
Kristiansen, Susan 59, 61
Kumar 125, 126

L
La Niña. see Alaya, Adriana Pérez
"labor pools" 188
Latinobarómetro 22, 132
Laughter 138–140, 166–167, 235
Lee Kuan Yew 87–88, 99–113, 115, 122–124, 126
Legal systems 53, 215
Leider, Richard 237–238
Liberal arts education 55, 69, 70–71
Life domains 211–212, 213, 214
Lin, Celina 88–91
Lithuania 132
Loma Linda, Calif. xi
Longevity x, xi, xii, 166
Lopez, Jesús 130
Lopez, Shane 241, 242
Lutherans 51, 124
Lyubomirsky, Sonja 9, 11, 12, 14, 16, 17, 19, 132

M
Malays 6, 95–98, 101, 102, 104
Malaysia 82, 87, 88, 101–102
Marriage 32–33, 228–229
Maryland 51
Maternity leave 217
Maxwell, Margaret 191

McKenry, Patrick 228
McLain, David 88
Mead, Leslie 182–186
Meditation 169, 234, 236, 245
Mexico 31, 129–171, 208, 212
  child healers 153–159
  crime 139, 148, 208
  family, importance of 147, 162, 170–171, 208, 225
  holidays 138, 148, 161
  humor 166–167, 208, 225
  job satisfaction 137, 220
  lessons from 165–171
  maternity leave 217
  police 135, 139–140, 141, 208
  religion and faith 147, 153, 162, 168–169, 208
  social interaction 169–170
Mexico City, Mexico 130–131, 136, 140–143, 160
Midnight sun 51
Mill, John Stuart 199
Mission Plaza, San Luis Obispo, Calif. 178, 190–195, 197, 200, 204
Mission statements, personal 237–238
moais 226–227
Moldova 18, 214
Money, happiness and 16–17, 48, 133–134, 146–147, 167–168, 210, 230
Montana 51

Index

Monterrey, Mexico 4, 130, 137, 138, 142–152, 165, 167
Mood, color and 236
Moody, Susan 46–47
Moreno, Alejandro 166
Mortgage payments 230–231
Munro, Jock 44, 45, 46, 47–48
Munro, Silvia 44, 45, 46
Music appreciation 35, 71, 208, 241
Music lessons 232, 241
Muslims 4, 7, 95–96, 97, 98
Myanmar 87

N
Nature, access to 52, 60, 64, 203
Netherlands 216
Nettle, Daniel 121
Nicholas, St. 51
Nicoya Peninsula, Costa Rica *x, xi,* 244
North Dakota 51
Norway 31
Nuevo León (state), Mexico *xiii,* 129, 139, 143, 144, 153, 154

O
Obama, Barack 100
Obesity 71, 196, 202, 242
Objective well-being 133, 134
Odder, Denmark 53, 54
Okinawa (island), Japan *xi*
    ancestor shrines 235
    moais 226–227

Online social networks 210
Ortiz, Claudia 156
Out-of-wedlock births 218
Oversocializing 169–170

P
Panama 31
Panchita *viii, ix–xi, xii, xiv,* 242–244
Papini, Giovanni 163
Paredón, Mexico 155, 159
Parental leave 43, 217
Parenthood 186, 230
Pedestrian malls 59, 216
People skills 239
Pet ownership 233–234
Philippines 124
Physical education 210, 242
Plotnikoff, Gregory 165–166
Political freedom 136, 215
Polls and surveys happiness measurement 21–22
Population density, happiness and 51
Potrero de Abrego, Mexico 163–164
Prayer 169, 229, 245
Pride shrines 235
Protestantism
    Denmark 42, 53, 68, 70
Puebla, Mexico 147, 148
Purpose partners 238

Q
Quality of life 11, 15, 22, 78, 200
Quit-smoking programs 201

R
Rademaker, Pierre 188–190, 201
Raffles, Sir Thomas Stamford 82
Raffles Holdings, Ltd. 92
Raffles Hotel, Singapore 91–92
Reiss, Jerry 195
Remembered happiness 169, 209
Retirement 69, 210, 231
Rosco, Roberto 156
Russia 18, 45, 91, 199

S
Safety, public 84, 85, 208, 217, 219
Saltillo, Mexico 159–161, 163
San Luis Obispo, Calif. *xiii,* 175–204, 208–209, 212
    antismoking policies 195, 201
    civic pride 204, 209
    farmer's market 181–182, 200
    job satisfaction 182, 184–185, 209, 220
    lessons from 200–204
    local wines 182–186, 209
    mission plaza project 178, 190–195, 197, 200, 204
    self-employment 188, 209

volunteering 182,
185, 209
Sandemose, Aksel 38
Sardinia (island), Italy *xi*
Savings accounts 231
Schwartz, Kenneth 175–
178, 188, 190–194,
199, 201, 203
Seasonal affective disor-
der 132, 236
Seidenfaden, Tøger
39–42
Self
as life domain 212
lessons in thriving
236–239
Self-employment 188,
209, 223
Serra, Junipero 175, 178
Shearer, Frank 165
Shopping hours 216
Sidewalks 203–204,
217, 218, 245
Sierra Leone 134
Signs, business 188,
201–202
Singapore *xiii*, 4, 6,
75–126, 166, 212
economic growth 86,
208
ethnic harmony 6,
84–85, 96, 124
family, importance of
84, 87, 105, 120,
126
law enforcement 78,
85, 111
lessons from 120–
126
mass participation
world records 97
millionaires 114
police 81, 92, 111,
124
safety and security
84, 85, 96, 120–
122, 208, 219

status equality
123–124
taxes 86, 87, 122,
123
upper class 89, 122
wage "top-up" policy
109, 123, 215
Singlish (dialect) 125
Sleep 236
Smoking 195–196, 201
Social life
as life domain 212
daily social time 137,
170, 221
lessons in thriving
224–230
online social
networks 210
see also Family;
Friends
Solis, Claudia 5, 8
South Dakota 51
South Korea 87
Southeast Asia 81, 83,
84, 92, 96
Sports 216, 226, 238,
242
Status equality 68, 219
Denmark 39, 68,
207, 219
Singapore 123–124
Stress hormones 233,
235
Suarez, Maria 156
Subjective well-being 80,
134, 168
Suicide 28, 36, 39, 132
Sunlight 132–133,
165–166, 235–236
Sunstein, Cass R. 232
Sutton, Remar 44–45,
47, 48
Sweden 31, 109
Swimming
cold-water swimming
36, 51, 71
Switzerland 31

T
Taiwan 87
Taliban 121
Talley Vineyards 182,
184, 185
Tan Ern Ser 83–85
Tanning 165
Taxes
Denmark 32, 33, 37,
42–43, 49, 70, 72
Mexico 166
Singapore 86, 87,
122, 123
Sweden 109
Teaching 223
Teenagers 218,
240–241, 242
Temkin, Benjamin
131–134
Thailand 87
Thaler, Richard 232
Thrive Centers 211–
212, 213, 214
Thriving, lessons in
community 214–219
financial life 230–232
home 232–236
self 236–239
social life 224–230
workplace 219–223
Tibetan monks 77, 169
Tlaxcala Indians 143
Tolstoy, Leo 199
Transparency Interna-
tional 84
Trujillo, Victor 140–141
TV viewing 210, 233

U
Ukraine 18
Unemployment 31, 86,
122, 215
United States
average annual
vacation days 41,
222, 232, 245

Index

average household
   debt 230, 231
civil rights 67
happiness ranking 31
least densely
   populated states
   51
least stressed states 51
marriage training
   programs 229
maternity leave 217
national happiness
   210
obesity rate 196
religion and faith 153
Uribe, Manuel 4–5, 7–8

V
Vacations 41, 70,
   221–222, 232, 245
VanderKelen, Barry
   196–197, 198
Veenhoven, Ruut 10,
   12, 21, 31, 77–79,
   228
Vietnam 87, 109
Vitamin D 132,
   165–166, 235–236
Volunteering 71, 72, 93,
   116, 185, 209, 210,
   239

W
Weber, Anders 25–29,
   36–38, 42, 44
Well-being
   objective 133, 134
   subjective 80, 134,
   168
Wildlife preserves 203
Wine, drinking 183
Wine industry 182–186
"workfare" 89, 123
Workplace
   as life domain 212

commuting 17, 150,
   189, 197, 221
home-based
   businesses 204
lessons in thriving
   219–223
see also Job
   satisfaction; Self-
   employment
Workweek, limiting
   216, 221
World
   happiest places 31
   unhappiest places 18
World Database of
   Happiness 10, 21,
   31, 100
World Health Organiza-
   tion 132
World Values Survey
   18, 21, 38, 84, 95,
   100, 125, 130, 132,
   133, 139
Wyoming 51

Y
Yusoh, Norridah 4, 6–7,
   98–99

Z
Zavala, Christina
   150–151
Zimbabwe 18